The Country Traveler

TIME-LIFE BOOKS

Alexandria, Virginia

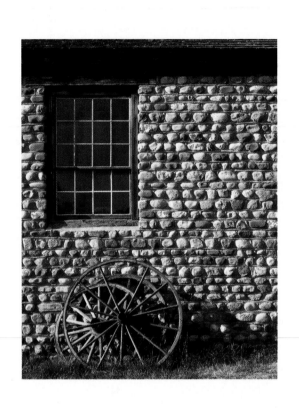

The Country Traveler

exploring the past at America's outdoor museums

A REBUS BOOK

C O N T E N T S

Ever since America's first outdoor museum was established in 1926 at Colonial Williamsburg, the restored capital of 18th-century Virginia, the public's imagination has been captured by the possibility of exploring an entire community that in effect exists in another time. There are now many such preservation projects located across America. Visitors to these sites are invited to enter early buildings—among them houses, taverns, shops, workplaces, and churches—and to experience a sense of the texture of everyday life through "displays" that involve everything from milking cows to cooking at the hearth.

This volume leads you on a tour of six outdoor museums that represent the diverse social, cultural, religious, and ethnic backgrounds of the country's settlers. Some of the museums consist of buildings restored on their original sites, and some are "approximations," created by bringing together early buildings, furnishings, tools, and other artifacts from a particular area. All have a remarkable story to tell.

Historic Deerfield in Massachusetts, for example, which comprises a dozen 18th- and 19th-century buildings and an extensive collection of early American decorative arts, offers insight into the surprisingly sophisticated tastes of the residents of one Connecticut River valley farm town. A far more simple, communal way of life is interpreted at Hancock Shaker Village, in Hancock, Massachusetts. This self-sufficient "City of Peace," as it was called in the 1800s, was once home to over two hundred members of the Shaker sect, religious separatists who gave up their property and worldly ties to devote their lives to God. The story of still another religious group, the Moravians, who established a thriving Church-run trade and crafts center in the North Carolina piedmont in 1766, is shared at Historic Old Salem.

By contrast, westward expansion is the focus of Genesee Country Museum in upstate New York. Here, more than fifty early buildings have been assembled to suggest the kind of frontier town that developed as farmers and entrepreneurs set out for the wilderness in search of new opportunities. Some westward-bound pioneers homesteaded in the Appalachian Mountains; both the difficulties and the pleasures of life in the isolated settlements of this region are recalled at the Museum of Appalachia, in northeastern Tennessee. And at El Rancho de las Golondrinas, near Santa Fe, New Mexico, visitors can experience yet another type of environment—one that recalls Spanish colonial life in the Southwest.

While time intentionally seems to stop at such museums, these places are by no means static institutions. Exhibitions, demonstrations, and interior furnishings are constantly being changed as new research helps to provide a more realistic perspective on the American past. Many outdoor museums also sponsor special educational programs, festivals, and seasonal celebrations, reinforcing the visitors' sense that they are traveling not only to a new place, but also to another era.

Historic Deerfield

*a prosperous farming village
preserved in the
Connecticut River valley*

The village of Deerfield, begun in 1669 as an outpost on the Massachusetts colony's western frontier, was twice destroyed by Indian massacres and abandoned by most of its inhabitants—in 1675 and in 1704. Perhaps as a result of this adversity, and the resolve of the settlers to re-establish their lives in the fertile Connecticut River valley, Deerfield residents became determined to protect their heritage. Some early villagers wrote accounts of their experiences, and saved and passed on their belongings to the next generations. In 1870, a historical association was formed, and the first restoration of an 18th-century Deerfield home took place twenty years later. By the 1940s, Henry and Helen Flynt, a couple interested in New England architecture and decorative arts, had started their own preservation effort, and in 1952 they assured Deerfield's future by creating a foundation honoring the town's past; the foundation was later named Historic Deerfield. *Continued*

The 1824 brick Wright House is one of Deerfield's most stately homes.

The curvaceous design of the gate above mirrors the scrolled pedimented doorways found on many Connecticut River valley homes.

The effects of the ongoing preservation effort in the town are visible today along the mile-long main thoroughfare, known simply as The Street since at least 1700. Canopied by stately maples, The Street is flanked by fifty-six buildings that date from the 18th to the early 19th centuries, giving the impression of a flourishing New England farm town that has changed little in modern times. The majority of the structures still serve as residences. Interspersed among them, however, are twelve buildings—including houses furnished to period, as well as a number of galleries exhibiting textiles, silver, and other decorative arts—that are owned by Historic Deerfield and are open to the public.

It is through the museum houses, in particular—and through the stories and eccentricities of the villagers who owned them—that Deerfield's early years come vividly to life. As the three restored residences on the following pages show,

Continued

Among the twelve museum buildings that line the main thoroughfare known as The Street is the circa 1725 Dwight-Barnard House, right.

The doorway on the circa 1730 Ashley House, above left, typifies the scroll-pedimented design indigenous to the Connecticut Valley; the entry on the 1743 Sheldon-Hawks House, above right, features a triangular pediment. The Georgian-period doors would have been added around 1760 to update the design of the homes.

the homes not only are invaluable examples of early New England architecture and interior decoration, but they also offer insight into American social history. The impressive doorways—designed to imitate expensive carved stone—as well as the fine appointments found inside the houses, indicate that early New England farmers could be quite sophisticated in their tastes and that they were extremely interested in keeping up with the styles of the time.

In the very early years, however, existence in Deerfield was rigorous. Living miles from Boston and other better established communities, the first residents were totally self-sufficient, dividing their energies between farming and defending themselves against Indian attack. In

the two massacres, more than one hundred villagers were slaughtered and an equal number led on a forced march to Canada. Yet those who survived the second massacre prevailed, and they eventually turned the rich soil of the river valley to their fortune, raising food crops and cattle and, later, in the 1800s, cash crops such as tobacco and broomcorn. After the Indian raids had subsided in the mid-18th century, the stability of the village was assured, and the prospering settlers were able to build spacious, comfortable homes for their families.

In restoring some of these houses, Historic Deerfield has attempted to present an accurate view of village life by preserving as much of the original character of the buildings as possible.

Many of the exteriors have survived relatively intact; where architectural elements were missing, as on several of the ornate doorways, contemporary reproductions were adapted from existing period examples. Early paint colors, discovered on clapboards, have also been matched.

Historical accuracy was an equally strong guiding force in the restoration of the interiors. Some furnishings have been passed down through generations of Deerfield residents and returned to their original settings, while others have been gathered from the surrounding area. In many cases, probate inventories—listings of household belongings that were customarily recorded after the death of a homeowner—as well as deeds, wills, diaries, account books, and oth-

er surviving documents, have made it possible to re-create rooms according to their specific uses and contents. In dwellings for which scant or no records exist, rooms have been turned into period showcases. These feature the type of furnishings that were found in early Deerfield homes, including carved chests, Chinese export porcelain, and elegant French wallpapers.

Although Historic Deerfield is committed to preservation, the village is not frozen in time. The interpretation of each residence is constantly evolving as new information comes to light about America's domestic history. Furnishings are changed and the core collections continue to be rearranged as assumptions about the past give way to a clearer understanding of it.

The brick door surround on the 1799 Asa Stebbins House, above left, shows a rusticated design, while the entry to the 1816 Wilson Printing Office, above right, features columnlike pilasters. The fanlights and the small windows were designed to help light the entry halls.

Jonathan Ashley, the town parson, used the parlor, right, for conducting such ministerial services as weddings and christenings; he also entertained company there. Among the sophisticated 18th-century furnishings in the room are a damask-covered Chippendale sofa, a claw-and-ball-foot "birdcage" tea table, and three carved cherry side chairs. The table and chairs are attributed to the noted Connecticut cabinetmaker Eliphalet Chapin.

Ashley House

Built between 1726 and 1733, the weathered clapboard residence at the north end of The Street was home to one of Deerfield's most prominent citizens—Parson Jonathan Ashley. A fiery preacher and an ardent supporter of the English Crown who was often locked out of his own church because of his Tory sympathies, Ashley lived in this handsome saltbox house until his death in 1780. In 1869, to make room for a "modern" Victorian dwelling, the house was moved by the clergyman's great-grandson to the rear of the property, where it served primarily as a tobacco barn.

Nearly eighty years later, the dilapidated house was brought back to its initial site at the front of the lot (its Victorian replacement was relocated down the street). It was then restored and furnished to an appearance believed to be appropriate to the parson's status and taste. Among the antiques displayed inside are locally made pieces, as well as some that have passed down through the Ashley family. The mix of furnishings, from the simple to the sophisticated, suggests that the parson was interested in acquiring new, fashionable pieces yet did not always part with what he already owned.

Continued

The Ashley House, above, built around 1726, features the tobacco-brown weathered clapboards and narrow nine-over-nine windows associated with 18th-century Deerfield homes. Parson Jonathan Ashley purchased the residence in 1733 for 251 pounds.

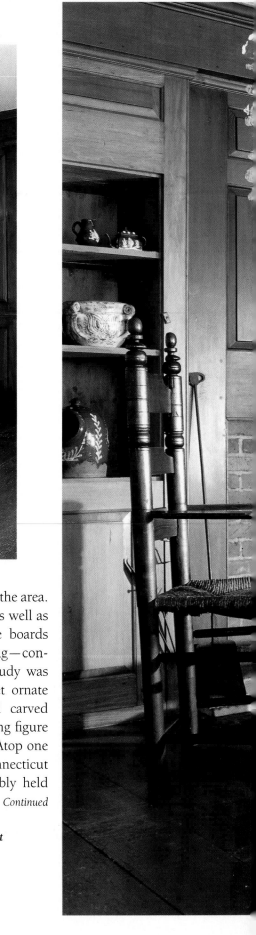

Architecturally, very little of the original house could be salvaged. On the exterior, the clapboards and windows were replaced and the doorway was reproduced from original colonial examples found in the Deerfield area. Of the interior, only one paneled wall in the parlor could be saved; the rest of the house was reconstructed according to period designs.

Representative of the restoration work that has been done in the house is an elegant fireplace surround in the parlor, featuring the columnlike carvings so often found on doorways of the area. In the stairwell and entry hall, above, as well as in the parson's study, right, old pine boards were used to re-create raised paneling—considered a luxury in the 1700s. The study was then filled with sturdy, functional, yet ornate furniture, including great chairs and carved stretcher-base tables of the type a leading figure in the community might have owned. Atop one of these tables, against a wall, is a Connecticut Valley oak Bible box that once probably held

Continued

Raised paneling crafted from old pine boards distinguishes the entrance hall, above, and the Loyalist parson's study, right; the 1772 mezzotint of King George III is an appropriate addition.

important papers. Inscribed 1681, it is the earliest dated piece in Historic Deerfield's collection.

One area of the house that has been returned to its original state on the basis of family expense accounts and locally recorded descriptions is the rear lean-to; the distinguishing feature of a salt-box house, it had been destroyed when the building was moved. As it did in Ashley's time, the lean-to now houses the kitchen, which is dominated by a cavernous cooking fireplace outfitted with iron trivets, frying pans, and other utensils. The fireplace also features an ingenious clock jack that once turned roasting spits via a complicated assemblage of gears. Most of the kitchen furnishings, including a rush-seated highchair and a carved pine cupboard, were col-

Continued

Removed from a house in Salem, Massachusetts, the built-in pine cupboard above is filled with 18th-century pottery, utensils, and pewterware. The sugar cone on the middle shelf, next to the sugar nippers, is typical of those imported from the West Indies.

Early utensils in the kitchen, left, include a cheese board (with a channel for whey), propped against a wall, and a candle dryer, hung above one window.

lected from the Deerfield area. However, the drop-leaf curly maple table was brought to the house by Dorothy Williams on her marriage to Ashley in 1736. The table is set as it may have been during the Ashleys' occupancy—with horn spoons, pewter plates, and wooden dishes.

Other important family pieces are displayed in an upstairs bedroom, or chamber, left: a chest-on-frame, found in the house when the structure was being used as the tobacco barn, and a set of linen bed hangings and a spread, embroidered in crewel by a cousin of the clergyman. The chamber, which was probably once crowded with several of Parson Ashley's nine children, is appointed with two large beds and a cradle; the plush bearskin rug and bright red wholecloth quilt suggest a taste for comfort and color.

The room is also filled with personal accessories that reveal something of the everyday customs of the adult occupants of the house. Next to the fireplace, for instance, are a wig stand and a rare chestnut cupboard with sliding doors made for storing several changes of wigs. And on the chest of drawers above sits a velvet cap that an 18th-century gentleman would have donned in the evening after shedding his wig.

The south chamber, left, contains an 18th-century canopy fold-up bed from the Connecticut Valley.
Displayed on the chest above are a pair of scissors and two primitive curling irons; the irons would have
been heated over a flame. Hanging on the wall is a "courting glass" made in the 1700s.

Frary House and Barnard Tavern

The Frary House and Barnard Tavern, an 18th-century house and tavern addition under the same roof, allow Historic Deerfield to show two interpretations of early village life side by side.

The double structure, above, and the property it stands on have an intriguing and convoluted history. It is known that Samson Frary, one of the village's first settlers, built a house on the lot in the late 1600s, but during the Indian massacre of 1704 most of his family was killed and the house destroyed. The earliest section of the structure that stands on the property today is marked by the central chimney and front door,

and is believed to have been erected in the 1760s by one of Frary's descendants. The tavern portion, located on the far end of the building, to the right of the front entry, was added in the 1790s, when the structure was owned by an innkeeper, Salah Barnard. After Barnard died in 1795, his widow inherited the house side of the building and his son Erastus received the "new" tavern. Located in the Barnard addition, the taproom, right, has been furnished to recall the character of 18th-century tavern life. It is in just such a room that villagers and stagecoach passengers would have gathered, with tankards and pipes in hand, for gossip and business dealings.

Continued

The street façade of the weathered structure above incorporates both the circa 1760s Frary House and the later Barnard Tavern addition, to the right of the entry. In the tavern section, the restored taproom, right, is furnished with Windsor chairs and a locally made Queen Anne table.

Furnished with a tip-top table and Chippendale chairs, the north parlor, above, is shown as C. Alice Baker restored it in the Colonial Revival style.

Passing from owner to owner over the next century, both the Frary House and the Barnard addition eventually fell into neglect. In 1890, C. Alice Baker, a descendant of Samson Frary, was encouraged by the town historian, George Sheldon, to purchase and save the derelict structure. Her decision to do so made her one of the earliest woman preservationists in America, and

the building was the first colonial house to be restored in Deerfield.

Converting the tavern portion to living quarters, Miss Baker focused her restoration on the Frary section of the building. Her interpretation reflects a romanticized notion of how the colonial settlers lived rather than a strict adherence to historical accuracy. Influenced by a contem-

This 1805 engraving, *Sailors Glee,* shows the patrons of a dockside tavern cavorting with women of questionable repute.

A typical tavern interior is shown in this 1813 painting by John Lewis Krimmel. The newspapers, kept on wall-mounted holders, were for use by patrons. The bar shelves hold decanters, punch bowls, glass tumblers, and pewter tankards.

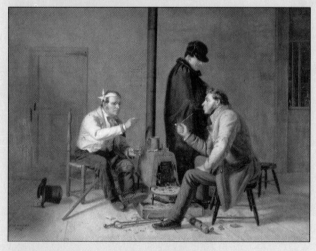

A Long Island tavern is the scene of this 1837 painting by William Sidney Mount. A barroom regular holds forth, while the pipe-smoking innkeeper and a caped traveler listen.

In this 1810 annotated drawing by Lewis Miller, Pennsylvania tavern keeper Martin Weiser is seen warming his feet on the stove while Mrs. Weiser serves customers.

Tavern keepers were required by law to use standard measures, like these quart, pint, and half-pint tankards.

Asa Stebbins House

In 1799, Asa Stebbins, a wealthy mill owner and farmer, built a brick residence, which was enlarged around 1810 with an imposing four-room addition that faced The Street. In effect, the remodeled house was a declaration of Stebbins's growing prosperity and status in the post-Revolutionary War period. The interior of the building was particularly fashionable, detailed with elegant moldings, mantels, and plasterwork trim in the then new, classically influenced Federal style, which was introduced to the Deerfield area by a well-known local architect, Asher Benjamin.

Because there is no record of the exact furnishings owned by the Stebbins family, the rooms have been decorated to suggest the taste of

Continued

A reflection of the owner's prosperity after the American Revolution, the Asa Stebbins House, above, begun in 1799, was the first brick residence in Deerfield. The Stebbins family, who were farmers and tanners, amassed much of their wealth by supplying leather goods for the Continental Army.

In the north parlor, left, the furnishings, including an upholstered lolling chair, a lady's desk, and a china tea set, indicate a gracious style of life.

31

any middle-class Deerfield family who might have favored the Federal style. In the elegant south parlor, right, for example, the windows are dressed with delicate embroidered curtains of mull—a type of thin muslin that was used at the time—and topped by tasseled brocade swags caught by moon-shaped tiebacks. Among the furnishings are period pieces, including shield-back chairs and a mahogany cylinder secretary with ivory pulls, from such style centers as Boston and New York City.

In addition to the textiles and furniture in the Stebbins House, the sophisticated wall treatments are also noteworthy. The entrance hall and stairwell, above, are decorated with French scenic wallpaper, which was particularly fashionable among the well-to-do in America in the early 19th century. The paper, made by a lead-

Continued

The work of local architect Asher Benjamin, who is pictured in the hallway portrait above, inspired the

elegant look of this house, exemplified by the staircase, and by the plaster trim in the south parlor,

right. Swag motifs, typical of the Federal style, are repeated throughout the parlor.

The wall decorations above have been restored to show off the original freehand brushwork. The designs were probably painted around 1812 by an itinerant artist named Jared Jessup, who worked in Connecticut and Massachusetts.

ing Parisian wallpaper company, Joseph Dufour et Cie., depicts the South Pacific voyages of Captain Cook; the design is complete with "savages" dressed in ancient Greek costume. The circa 1804 wallpaper was salvaged by Historic Deerfield earlier in this century from the Ruel Williams Mansion in Augusta, Maine, before that residence was demolished. Other distinctive wall decorations in the Stebbins house include freehand-painted borders that date to the early 1800s; these have been carefully restored to match their original colors.

The dining room of the Stebbins House—perhaps the first such room in Deerfield—also suggests the new, more gracious way of life that emerged after the Revolution. As families prospered, they began to turn rooms to a single

Continued

In the dining room, right, the mahogany table and sideboard, both from Massachusetts, are set with elegant Chinese export porcelain.

use and fill them with the stylish furniture, like sideboards and serving tables, that was beginning to be created for such specific purposes. The fine materials from which these new pieces were made, including inlaid and veneered mahogany, are evident in the furnishings showcased in the Stebbins dining room. Also on display is an extensive set of Chinese export porcelain, popular among the wealthy in the early 1800s.

Amenities found in the upstairs bedrooms continue to suggest the comforts that a family like the Stebbinses could have enjoyed. In the south chamber, left, for instance, a minutely carved ivory chess set from China indicates an interest in—and the time for—leisure activities. The decorated looking glasses in the north chamber, above, would have been considered luxury items of particular value. In the same room, the tasseled silk curtain swags and the embroidered bed valance made of Chinese silk were fashioned especially to coordinate with the ornate pattern of the French wallpaper.

Fine bed linens and French wallpapers distinguish the two upstairs bedrooms. The south chamber, left, features a candlewick spread and trompe l'oeil wall drapery that was inspired by Napoleon's campaign tents. In the north chamber, above, the wallpaper also bears a swag motif.

THE FEDERAL STYLE

Decoration of the American home in the decades following the Revolution was affected by two related trends: the surge of patriotism after the war and an interest in ancient cultures prompted by current archaeological discoveries in Italy and Greece.

In establishing the new nation, George Washington and Thomas Jefferson looked to classical civilizations, admired for their democratic traditions, as models, and promoted a neoclassical style for early government buildings. Both the architecture and the decorative arts produced in what is now known as the Federal period—from about 1790 to 1820—incorporated design motifs like those found in ancient Rome and Greece. These include such classical elements as urns, lyres, swags, cornucopias, acanthus leaves, wheat sheaves, and the eagle, an ancient symbol of power.

In particular, furniture makers and other craftsmen in urban centers such as Boston, Baltimore, and Phil-adelphia, featured classically inspired motifs in the pieces they made. Chairs might have shield-shaped backs, with splats carved into urn designs, and seat upholstery fastened with brass nails aligned in a swag pattern. Tables and chests often had brass drawer pulls fashioned into rosettes or lions' heads.

The Federal style affected the look not just of furniture, but of all the elements of a room's decor, lending interiors a unified appearance for the first time. For instance, wallpaper was decorated with images of festoons and laurel wreaths. Paintings, engravings, and sculptures, also based on classical sources, often depicted allegorical scenes or toga-clad figures. Elements from classical architecture frequently served as inspiration: candlesticks and vases were set atop pedestals, and columns and pediments were adapted for fireplace surrounds and for mirror frames, which were often further embellished with gilt, a finish used by the ancient Greeks.

The furnishings at right exhibit the classical motifs and the light, symmetrical, geometric look typical of the Federal period.

Genesee
Country Museum

*the spirit of a growing
frontier settlement captured
in upstate New York*

G enesee, an Indian word that means "pleasant valley," was an apt choice of name for the region
of northwest New York State that stretches from
Seneca Lake to Niagara Falls. Acquired from the
Iroquois by eastern land companies in the decades after the
Revolutionary War, the area was known for its dense forests
and rolling hills, and was among the first territories to be set-
tled as America began to expand westward. By the mid-1800s,
it had evolved from a pioneer encampment into a center of
commerce. An important part of American history, this rapid
development—typical of many frontier regions—is the focus of
Genesee Country Museum in Mumford, New York.

Set on two hundred acres of farmland crisscrossed by garden
plots, winding dirt roads, and split-rail fences, the museum
features a village of some fifty early buildings that have been

Continued

Cows laze by 19th-century farm buildings at Genesee Country Museum.

moved from surrounding towns and restored. No single frontier village has been reproduced; instead, the structures, which include a tavern, a town hall, and schools, as well as the shops of various merchants, are meant to capture the general character of early settlements in the area known as Genesee Country. To that end, offices of individuals who played important roles in small-town life—the doctor, lawyer, and land agent—can also be found, along with workshops of such craftsmen as the tinsmith and the potter. In addition, there are several period houses, which, ranging from a rudimentary cabin to a Victorian mansion, help to chronicle the evolution of architectural styles in the area. Furnished to period, the houses also reflect how the needs and tastes of the settlers changed as their quality of life improved.

Lured by land speculators, these early settlers from New England, Pennsylvania, and the South included not only farmers, but also craftsmen and merchants eager to offer their services to fellow pioneers. The newcomers cleared their own land, planted crops, and lived in cabins until they could afford to build better houses.

After about 1810, improved roads hastened settlement and made it possible to send profit-able shipments of lumber and grain to eastern cities. With the 1825 opening of the Erie Canal, the earlier, pioneer era was gone forever; goods could be shipped in by barge at a fraction of the cost of overland travel, and canal boats—and soon, railroads—made it easier to travel west. Thousands of people did so, and many disembarked in Genesee Country, quickly turning villages into towns, and towns into cities.

The clapboard tavern, town hall, and female seminary above typify the 19th-century buildings that were found in the pioneer towns of Genesee Country.

A Genesee settler named Nicholas Hetchler erected the log cabin above in 1806; the squared oak timbers reflect a building tradition of his native Pennsylvania. The 1830 blacksmith's shop, right, is an example of cobblestone architecture, which is indigenous to upstate New York.

The printer's shop, above, was created from two smaller, separate shops. The simpler rear portion dates to around 1820, while the Greek Revival front section was built in 1835; both originally stood in Caledonia, New York. When the Federal-style house at left was built by mill owner John McKay around 1814, it was one of the most stylish homes in that same town.

COBBLESTONE BUILDINGS

Dating from about 1825 to 1860, the remarkable mansonry buildings shown here are constructed with cobblestones in a decorative technique that is indigenous to the Lake Ontario region near Rochester, New York. Although the glacially deposited cobblestones are found elsewhere in America, their use as a building material was initially limited to upstate New York. After completing the Erie Canal there in 1825, thousands of masons—many from Europe—sought more work in the area. When they began erecting farmhouses, churches, schools, and shops faced with the stones, the craftsmen may have been continuing a tradition that existed in their own homelands.

The first buildings the masons put up were made of field cobblestones in varying sizes and shapes. But gradually the craftsmen began to select more uniform stones, favoring the rounded, water-washed cobbles found on the shores of Lake Ontario.

While horizontal patterns were the most common, the masons also created vertical and diagonal designs, and an interesting herringbone variation was achieved by setting oval stones at an angle. Little is known, however, about how cobblestone walls were actually constructed; intense competition caused most of the masons to keep their techniques secret.

An 1849 schoolhouse features a particularly uniform horizontal cobble pattern.

A diagonal design distinguishes the masonry of an 1846 farmhouse.

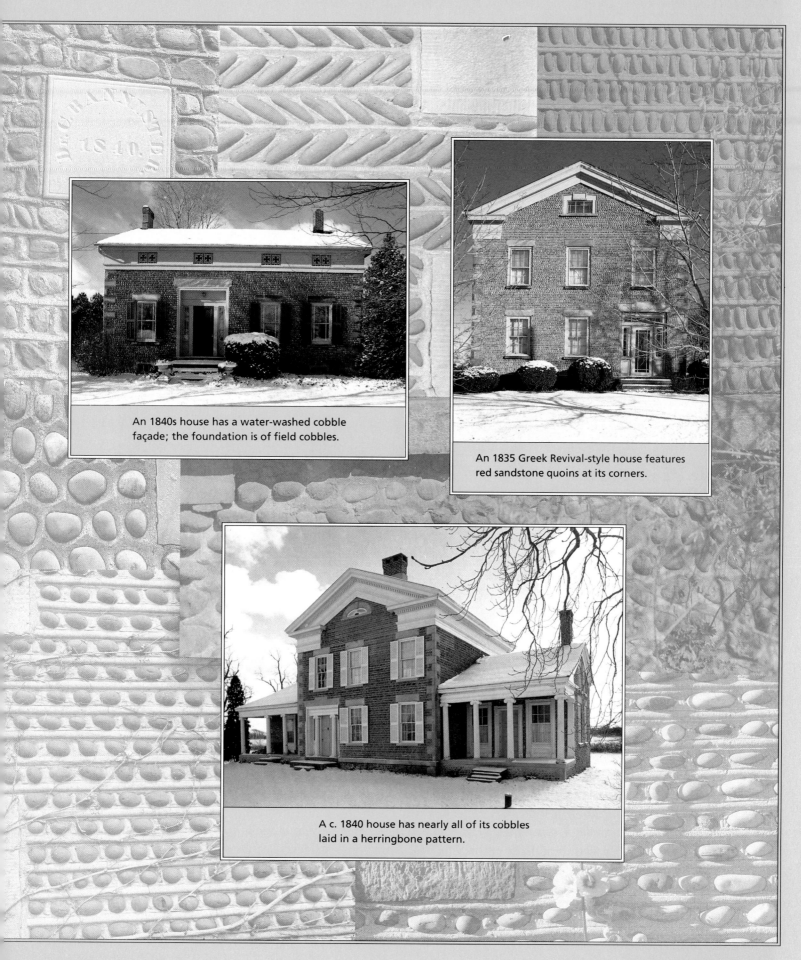

An 1840s house has a water-washed cobble façade; the foundation is of field cobbles.

An 1835 Greek Revival-style house features red sandstone quoins at its corners.

A c. 1840 house has nearly all of its cobbles laid in a herringbone pattern.

Amherst Humphrey House

The 1797 Amherst Humphrey homestead, above, is one of the oldest houses at Genesee Country Museum. It was used continuously as a farmhouse for 175 years before being moved to the museum grounds.

When Amherst Humphrey built his ten-room frame house in Lima, New York, in 1797, it must have stood in marked contrast to the log homes of his neighbors. While the residence probably seemed fashionable in pioneer territory, its architecture actually echoed that of houses built a century earlier in New England. Humphrey came from Massachusetts and quite logically re-created the kind of home that was already familiar to him.

Although the house is almost austere in its simplicity, it is nevertheless trimmed inside and out with beautifully planed moldings and paneled doors. The mantelpieces, chair rails, and built-in cupboards are also the work of skilled hands, and display a careful attention to detail. Such features were rare in a region where settlement had begun only a few years earlier, and where rustic shelters were the best that the majority of settlers could hope for.

Humphrey, however, evidently fared better than some. Although details about his life are scarce, it is known that he was a farmer and probably grew wheat in the fields that he had cleared himself. It is estimated that a man could single-handedly cut down ten acres of woods in a year, although he would require help when it came to clearing away the felled trees.

Humphrey could probably afford that help; a stone fireplace in the basement of the house sug-

Continued

The front door opens into a small stair hall, left, a typical feature of the center-chimney plan on which the house design was based. The simple woodwork recalls that of earlier houses in Massachusetts, Humphrey's native state.

Scissorlike candle snuffers like the late-18th-century piece above were used to extinguish a candle's flame and to trim the wick; the small box at the end of the blade would catch the cut-off portion. Important household utensils, snuffers were often made in sets with a matching tray and candlestick.

gests that he, like many other farmers in the area, earned extra income by burning his excess wood and converting the ashes into potash, or lye. Potash, then used in the manufacture of such products as glass, soap, and bleach, could be sold in East Coast cities for as much as two hundred dollars a ton, a sum that would easily allow a farmer to take on a hired hand for a year.

Amherst Humphrey designed his new house in a basic building plan that revolved around a massive central chimney. Even without fireplaces of their own, the rooms abutting the brick chimney received residual warmth from the kitchen's hearth fire and oven. Indeed, on the second floor, only the largest of the five

bedrooms—which were evidently shared by Humphrey's nine children—features a fireplace. As was typical of most homes of the period, a first-floor parlor doubled as the master bedroom.

The rooms reflect the simple comforts of a prosperous country family of the early 1800s; most of the furnishings are from New England and date from the mid-1700s to the first decades of the 19th century. This suggests that the Humphreys brought their belongings with them when they moved to Genesee Country from New England, and did not purchase new pieces, such as rag rugs—typically sold by itinerant weavers—and stenciled chairs, until they could more easily afford them.

The sitting room, above, is set up for dining. The Queen Anne table and the banister-back chairs, which were probably made in Connecticut in the late 1700s, are the type of furnishings the Humphreys presumably brought to Genesee Country from New England.

The front parlor, opposite, contains a Federal-period tester bed. The embroidered homespun blanket of woven wool is a reproduction of a 19th-century blanket in the museum's collection.

Foster-Tufts House

Farmer Charles Foster and his family had lived west of the Genesee River in Pavilion, New York, for ten years when he replaced their log cabin with a large frame house in 1836. The column-like pilasters, large windows, end chimneys, center-hallway plan, and deeply carved interior moldings are all typical of the Federal style that had been popular back East through the 1820s. The deep overhang of the roof, however, shows a familiarity with the new Greek Revival style, suggesting that Foster was interested in keeping up with the times—even if the times came fifteen or twenty years later for a backwoods farmer on the frontier.

The house, apparently the first of its type in the Pavilion area, was thus quite sophisticated for the region. And while it displays stylistic conventions transplanted from New England, it also exhibits a good deal of originality on the part of the builder, who clearly had ideas of his own. The front doorway, for example, with fluted pilasters framing a second-story window, is the only such design known in the area. And inside can be found some unusual additions to the center-hallway plan, including a slipper room—a small chamber, adjacent to the parlor, that was perhaps used by an elderly family member—and an arched alcove, just large enough for a bed, off the dining room.

Foster's house eventually passed to a daugh-

Continued

The Foster-Tufts House, above, was built in 1836 and displays an end-chimney design typical of the Federal period. The wallpaper, window valances (copied from an 1838 decorating book called The Workwoman's Guide)*, and floor cloth in the parlor, left, are conservative, yet stylish for the time.*

The dining room alcove, above, may have been a borning room. The cotton bedspread, stenciled with twenty-six different designs, is a reproduction of a circa 1830 piece.

ter, who married a local man named Ely Tufts, and it remained in the Tufts family for three generations; the restoration brings it back to its 1836 appearance. By that date the Erie Canal had been in operation for eleven years, and mule-drawn canal barges were bringing regular shipments of goods to the area from eastern cities. It was now a simple matter for homeowners like the Foster family to order furniture, and for

Continued

Furnishings such as the Empire-style chairs, table, and mirror in the dining room, right, reflect an interest in current styles of the 1830s.

During the days of frontier settlement, candles were usually made at home from tallow, or rendered animal fat, and stored in wall boxes. This box of carved white pine was made in Connecticut around 1790.

shopkeepers to stock a ready supply of wall-papers and fabrics. The first American do-it-yourself home decorating books also appeared during this period, and these were full of information on the latest color schemes and window treatments. Thus, no matter how far homeowners were from a city, they could stay abreast of current decorating styles.

Despite its up-to-date look, however, there are signs that the house belonged to a farmer rather than to a wealthy businessman, who might have lived in a more prosperous town in the area. The furniture is simple and sturdy, and most pieces are country versions of the more costly high-style pieces that would also have been available. The grass mats, floor cloths, and rag rugs found throughout the house were far less expensive than carpeting, and were easier to keep clean. These, like the stenciled coverlets and pieced quilts in the bedrooms, recall the work of a farmer's wife who was careful with her pennies, yet still proud of her home.

At the kitchen hearth, left, a pieced bedcover is stretched on a quilting frame. The kitchen
wares on the pantry shelves, above, include baskets and pottery typically used in the early 1800s,
as well as a rare 19th-century redware mold made in the shape of a fish.

Livingston-Backus House

An imposing door, distinguished by egg-and-dart molding, opens to the entryway, right. Tiebacks like the large brass rosettes gathering the curtains were standard accessories for well-dressed windows during the 1830s.

While Genesee Country represented opportunity to farmers moving west, it also had much to offer astute businessmen who were quick to profit from land speculation, as well as from the new trade made possible by the 1825 opening of the Erie Canal. James Livingston, an entrepreneur in Rochester, New York, had made a fortune from his investments in milling, banking, and speculative ventures when, around 1827, he built his Greek Revival mansion.

Livingston's choice of architectural styles for one of Rochester's first important houses is indicative of the times. To America's young re-public of the 1820s, the Greek Revival symbolized the democratic ideals of classical antiquity and marked an important break with the English architecture that was used throughout the colonial and Federal periods. Hallmarks of the style, the pedimented porch and classical columns on Livingston's house not only were in the height of fashion, they also made the building appear as a splendid temple: testimony to the owner's financial success.

Originally grand, Livingston's house became even grander in the hands of a later owner, Frederick Backus, a Rochester civic leader and physician who purchased the residence in 1835 for

Continued

The Livingston-Backus House, above, was built in the Greek Revival style in 1827, and was enlarged with a rear wing and side portico between 1838 and 1840. During the late 19th and early 20th centuries, it was used as a girls' school, known as Livingston Park Seminary.

Reflecting classical design motifs, the 1830s newel post at the foot of the staircase, above, is carved with pineapple and acanthus ornamentation.

ten thousand dollars. Backus made substantial alterations, adding a one-story addition to the rear of the house, then moving the entrance to the side, under a columned portico.

The new owner also updated the interior. A formal entryway complete with a graceful staircase—which no doubt made a suitable impression—was created, and the parlor was doubled in size. As was the custom of the day, this room had sliding doors that could be closed to make two cozier spaces or opened to create a spacious room for a large party.

Complete with its additions, the house is now furnished to look as it might have in Backus's time. His taste was thoroughly in keeping with the Greek Revival style—which remained popular into the 1840s. As was often the case during the period, the favored decorative motifs were

not strictly Greek in origin, but more generally "classical." Many wallpapers were printed with trompe l'oeil designs that effectively simulated the appearance of marble walls, carved architectural friezes, or graceful draperies. At the windows, gauzy white curtains were swept into folds with silk cords, and topped with swag valances. Chandeliers and wall sconces were designed after ancient bronze lighting fixtures, while patterned carpets were woven to resemble Roman tile floors.

Even the fashionable furniture of the day—popularized by such contemporary designers as Duncan Phyfe and Charles-Honoré Lannuier, and produced in New York, Baltimore, and other East Coast cities—was classically inspired. The most popular chair form of the period featured saber-shaped legs that curved in oppos-

Continued

Sliding doors open to create the double parlor above, where silk-screened wallpaper recalls the French papers that were fashionable in America in the early 1800s.

ing directions like those of its prototype, the Greek klismos chair. Motifs such as acanthus leaves or animal heads and paws were used in carved decoration, and scaled-down architectural columns were likely to trim secretaries and console tables. This classical furniture was large in its proportions, to fit the scale of rooms in Greek Revival houses, and the decorating look was balanced; furniture could now be bought in suites, to produce a harmonious room.

The impressive formality of the period also extended to landscape design, exemplified by the Livingston-Backus garden. Laid out in a symmetrical pattern behind the house, the garden features a network of brick walks that intersect beds of flowers and shrubs edged with boxwood; the columned pergola, or shaded walkway, at one end owes its origins to ancient Rome. A garden such as this one, in a town that only twenty years earlier had been a wilderness settlement, would have been a true mark of civilized living, and a clear statement that Rochester's leading citizens were as worldly and up-to-date as anyone in the East.

Located in the rear of the house, the kitchen, above, has a rustic look in comparison with that of the formal front rooms. A cook and serving maid, however, would have been in residence to prepare and present such elegant dishes as tea cakes and fruit tarts.

*Classically inspired pergolas
like the one in the Livingston-
Backus garden at left were
much in vogue in the 1830s.
Wisteria forms a canopy
over the top.*

63

The Drugstore

A trade sign in the form of a mortar and pestle calls attention to the wares sold at the circa 1840 drugstore above. With its columned "temple" front, the building typifies the small-town versions of the Greek Revival style that proliferated in the area.

The little drugstore at Genesee Country Museum was originally built around 1840 to serve the community of Tyrone, New York. Although pharmacists at the time were seldom trained as chemists, they nevertheless prepared and dispensed a wide range of remedies. Along with the special prescriptions that they weighed out on scales and mixed with a mortar and pestle, these versatile shopkeepers also sold popular varieties of patent medicines, such as coughdrops, corn plasters, and syrups, as well as perfumes and painting supplies.

The apothecary chests at right contain plants such as smartweed and skunk cabbage, once deemed necessary for effective cures.

QUACKERY

While drugstores thrived in the 18th and 19th centuries, so did the business of quackery. In a time when medical treatment was usually gruesome, expensive, and ineffective, charlatans selling so-called quick cures found a ready market for nostrums and gadgets said to remedy everything from "female complaints" to cancer.

Among the most popular quack cures were patent medicines, largely worthless elixirs, balms, and pills that could be purchased without a prescription. The business of selling patent medicines was flourishing in England, and imports had become quite popular in America by the 1750s. The first American patent for a medicine was registered in 1796 by Samuel Lee, Jr., the inventor of "Bilious Pills." Lee's pills were evidently quite versatile, as they were sold as a cure not only for biliousness, but also for yellow fever, jaundice, and dysentery. By contrast, "Dr." Thomas W. Dyott, the druggist's apprentice who in the early 1800s became the country's first patent medicine magnate, successfully marketed a remedy for "a certain disease" that was never named at all.

Countless variations on such quack cures were widely available at medicine shows and in all manner of shops—including drugstores, where the counters were piled high

with convincing propaganda. "Thousands have a premature death from the want of a little attention to the common cold," read one ad for an expectorant syrup called "Last Day." Such declarations might be backed up by claims of dependability, em-

This sheet music is for an 1887 song parodying quacks; sarsaparilla was used in some patent medicines.

phasized in product names such as "Warner's Safe Cure" and "Comstock's Dead Shot Pellets." A touch of the exotic also helped sales: "South American Fever and Ague Remedy" and "Carpathian Bitters" were just two of the many "international" cures available.

In addition to patent medicines,

those suffering from various ailments—including the dreaded tuberculosis—could choose from such novel products as "Waterproof Anti-Consumptive Cork Soles" (worn in the shoes), "Medicated Fur Chest Protectors," and the "Quassia Cup."

The latter was made from the wood of the tropical quassia tree, which was believed to have medicinal properties that were imparted to whatever was drunk from the cup. To ease pain, one might try "metallic tractors," which supposedly drew harmful electricity from the body. Other imaginative "cures" included electromagnetic belts, garters, and corsets, and the frightening "Baunscheidt" device, which, by blistering the skin, was said to rid the system of infection.

While countless consumers fell for such quack remedies, the lack of a scientific basis for the "cures" did not go unnoticed. Providing a rich source of material for satirical songwriters and printmakers, quacks were also seriously criticized by politicians and physicians. Reform was ever a subject of debate, and by the early 1900s stricter regulations governing the medicine industry signaled the beginning of the end for quackery.

Among the quack inventions opposite are 19th-century patent medicines, electric shock machines, and a "Quassia Cup."

The interior of the store, right, probably looks much as it did when the building was erected in 1848. The shelves hold bolts of fabric, buttons, thread, and other sewing goods; cheese strainers and baskets hang from the beams.

The Altay Store

The general store was central to small-town life in 19th-century America. In fact, on many country roads, the appearance of a store might well have been the only signal to visitors that they were in a town at all.

The first general store in Altay, a tiny village in New York's Finger Lakes region, opened for business in 1819. In 1848, the enterprise was moved into a new building, where it remained until it closed down in 1899. As restored today, the 1848 structure retains its original built-in cupboards, shelves, and counters, and displays an accurate inventory of wares, assembled according to the store's mid-19th-century ledgers.

As the broad selection of goods reveals, nearly everything a homeowner might need from day to day could be found at a general store. Since

Continued

A general store was the town hub, where local residents caught up on news. Bulletin boards like the one outside the Altay Store, above, kept villagers abreast of current events, even when business hours were over.

Improved printing methods made wallpaper widely accessible in the 1840s, and displays like the one above could be found in many small-town stores.

nothing was prepackaged, the interior was apt to be permeated with the mixed aromas of tobacco, cheddar cheese, lamp oil, molasses, and roasted coffee beans, which sat on shelves and in kegs ready to be measured out and taken home. The shelves were also filled with bolts of fabric, non-perishable foods, razor blades, hardware, harnesses, tableware, hats, shoes, wallpaper, and soap. And if the shopkeeper still lacked an item a customer wanted, he would search for it on his next trip to the city.

In spite of their varied and sought-after inventory, the proprietors of general stores rarely grew rich. In fact, because most business was transacted on credit, they often barely made ends meet. In the early days, local residents might bring by wagonloads of baskets or pottery, several bushels of potatoes, or a tub of fresh

butter to barter for something they needed, and it was customary to run up large bills. These were paid only at harvest time when there was cash on hand.

As a result, shop owners had to be diligent bookkeepers, keeping track of what was owed to them and when the money was promised. Many proprietors also functioned as small-town bankers, locking up their neighbors' savings in their safes. The stores also often doubled as post offices; some had a pigeonhole letter box for each local resident, which made it easy for everyone else in town to see just who had received mail. The general store was also a lively community center, where politics was discussed and news and gossip exchanged, and where friends could meet to play a game of checkers near the potbellied stove.

General stores were the start of one-stop shopping. At the Altay Store, above, patrons could buy lamp chimneys, yellowware, and packets of Dr. Morse's Indian Root Pills.

Tinsmith's Shop

In the 19th century, the products made by tinsmiths were important additions to the household. At this time, what was called tin was actually thin sheet iron plated with tin to protect against rust. The lightweight, durable material was easily cut, bent, riveted, and soldered, and when new it featured a bright, shiny surface that made it an inexpensive substitute for pewter.

In most communities tin goods were bought ready-made from peddlers, who carried their wares from town to town in horse-drawn carriages. In several Genesee Country villages, however, tinsmiths set up shop and sold their products on site. Typical of such an enterprise, the Tinsmith's Shop at Genesee Country Museum is outfitted with a workbench, tinsmithing tools, and a wide assortment of 19th-century tin household goods; hanging from a rafter is an unusual tin rocking chair, crafted around 1865 in Elba, New York, in honor of a couple's tenth anniversary (symbolized by tin).

The greater the range of goods an individual could produce for the home and farmyard, the more his skills were in demand. The successful tinsmith, consequently, was usually a versatile craftsman. He made a diverse selection of utilitarian objects, such as candle molds, measuring cups, buckets, and oilcans, as well as lighting devices—including candlesticks, pierced lanterns, and chandeliers that were attractive enough for use in the parlor.

The building housing the Tinsmith's Shop, above, dates to 1860. Among the 19th-century tin wares displayed inside, at right, are pierced lanterns and a rather elegant chandelier; the smith's tools include an anvil, as well as edging, crimping, and shearing devices.

The Museum of Appalachia

a Tennessee mountain village
rich in pioneer history

Settlement in the Appalachian Mountain region of northern Tennessee began in the late 1700s as homesteaders arrived from Pennsylvania, Virginia, and the Carolinas to start new lives. Both the hardships and pleasures experienced by these pioneers, romanticized in tales of familiar frontier figures like Davy Crockett and Daniel Boone, now seem part of the distant past. Yet, in much of the southern highlands region of Appalachia—which stretches from northern Alabama up to Maryland—it was not until the 1930s that life changed markedly from the early days. Modern ways were slow to reach the isolated mountain settlements, where family customs, as well as traditional methods of handcraftsmanship and farming, held fast, passing unchanged from one generation to the next.

The distinctive character of this pioneer heritage is recalled at the Museum of Appalachia in Norris, Tennessee, where dozens of log buildings from the region are assembled, including a

Continued

Typically kept by mountain families for food and wool, sheep graze near a haystack.

gristmill, a church, a school, barns, smokehouses, and cabins, all dating from the late 1700s to the early 1900s. Here, on sixty-five acres of woods and pasture, life easily returns to the days when fiddle music floated through the poplar trees and evenings were spent spinning yarns on the front porch.

Scattered throughout the property, the houses—filled with simple, handmade furniture, and the tools and cooking utensils that were necessities in every household—appear as though their residents have just stepped out for a moment. In fields and barnyards, shingle splitting, molasses making, and other activities take place, while sheep, mules, pigs, and oxen graze behind split-rail fences. Each spring, old varieties of fruit trees blossom in an orchard. And each fall, cabbages and turnips are harvested from a vegetable garden and then buried—following local custom—in leaf-lined holes, to be preserved for use in the winter.

Originally owned by local families, the buildings, tools, and household implements that are used to suggest Appalachian life were collected and moved to the site by John Rice Irwin, who opened the museum in 1969 and still oversees it. A descendant of pioneers himself, Irwin grew up on a Tennessee farm and developed a fascination with Appalachian life during his boyhood. Since then he has traveled miles of mountain road searching for such artifacts as thistle hoes, flyminders, and bark grinders, and for the stories—often as curious as the names—that go with them. Presented in the context of living Appalachian history, such finds are more than outmoded tools and household conveniences;

Continued

The porch of the Peters Homestead, left, overlooks the sheep meadow and cow pasture. The cabin above is said to have been built by the Patterson family, who were among the region's first settlers.

they represent the self-sufficiency of a mountain people whose isolation and poverty left them little to rely on beyond their own ingenuity and a deep knowledge of nature.

By the time many pioneers arrived in the region, the choice acreage in the bottomlands and foothills had already been sold, and the mountains offered the only available, or affordable, land. While homesteaders could raise enough food to support a family there, the steep slopes made it nearly impossible to grow wheat or corn as cash crops, and settlers were often reduced to subsistence living. Yet, many stayed, cherishing both their isolation and the freedom that it afforded them.

That these proud and resourceful people literally lived off the land may best be seen, perhaps, in their modest dwellings. Poplars, which

grow tall and straight, yielded the wood commonly used for the log cabins of the region, while sandstone and limestone were shaped into chimneys and fireplaces. (Limestone worked particularly well because it could easily be cut into bricklike shapes, simplifying construction.) The mortar used for masonry and for chinking logs was mixed from mud; the trick here was in learning what type of mud to use.

The settlers did learn, and, fortunately, first-hand knowledge of their old building methods, as well as a familiarity with such crafts as coopering and basketmaking, was still available when the museum was founded. As a result, a sense of authenticity colors the displays and activities here, and these in turn reveal much about local mountain culture while telling the larger story of frontier settlement.

The top section of the Wilson Barn, above, was designed to store hay and corn fodder, while the overhang on one side made a convenient shelter.

The mule-powered cane press, above, is used for making molasses; the gourds hanging from poles serve as birdhouses for the purple martins that take up residence each spring. The shed at right houses the tools used by the wheelwright, the blacksmith, and the miller, three of the most important tradesmen in a frontier settlement.

The cantilevered barn above, moved from a farm in Sevier County, Tennessee, exemplifies a type of architecture peculiar to eastern Tennessee and western North Carolina. The Peters Homestead, left, which may date to the 1790s, is the only two-story dwelling at the museum. Nathaniel Peters moved in with his bride in 1838, and the house remained in the family until the 1940s.

A SENSE OF PLACE

The writings of novelist and poet James Still are strongly identified with the southern highlands region of Appalachia, which stretches from northern Alabama up to Maryland. The characters in his books often speak in the local idiom, and the imagery frequently evokes the Appalachian hills and rivers, both powerful symbols of beauty and endurance.

Still, who was born in 1906 in Lafayette, Alabama, and now lives near Wolfpen Creek in eastern Kentucky, has spent his career as a writer, librarian, and professor of English. His early books were part of the great outpouring of southern literature in the 1920s and 1930s, which also included the works of Thomas Wolfe and Robert Penn Warren.

Particularly evocative of Still's adopted Appalachian hills, the poem "Heritage," below, written around 1930, expresses a strong sense of place. In this piece, the author speaks of a land well known to people like those pictured at right—a land where old values, old traditions, and old ways of life lingered long after they had disappeared in other parts of the nation.

The proprietor of Johnson's Store, near Sneedville, Tennessee, takes her ease at the doorway; c. 1950.

Ila Mae Martin by her root cellar, where vegetables and dairy products were stored; c. 1968.

HERITAGE

I shall not leave these prisoning hills
Though they topple their barren heads to level earth
And the forests slide uprooted out of the sky.
Though the waters of Troublesome, of Trace Fork,
Of Sand Lick rise in a single body to glean the valleys,
To drown lush pennyroyal, to unravel rail fences;
Though the sun-ball breaks the ridges into dust
And burns its strength into the blistered rock
I cannot leave. I cannot go away.

Being of these hills, being one with the fox
Stealing into the shadows, one with the new-born foal,
The lumbering ox drawing green beech logs to mill,
One with the destined feet of man climbing and descending,
And one with death rising to bloom again, I cannot go.
Being of these hills I cannot pass beyond.

Hobart Hoskins plays a trumpet that he made himself from a homegrown gourd; 1960.

The stick-and-mud chimney on this cabin in Harriman, Tennessee, was deliberately designed to lean. If the chimney caught fire, the prop pole could be quickly removed so that the burning chimney would fall away from the house; c. 1900.

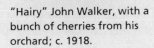

"Hairy" John Walker, with a bunch of cherries from his orchard; c. 1918.

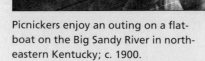

Picnickers enjoy an outing on a flatboat on the Big Sandy River in northeastern Kentucky; c. 1900.

Dollie Turnbill, age eighty-six, with an egg basket given to her when she was a child; 1980.

A mule-drawn school wagon carries a full load of children to classes in Anderson County, Tennessee; c. 1920.

McClung House

The McClung House, above, is thought to have been built in the 1790s, and originally stood a few miles southwest of what is now Knoxville. Its two rooms are separated by a dogtrot, or breezeway, but are covered by a single roof.

The Knoxville area of Tennessee, just south of Norris, was little more than wilderness when the McClung family built a log home there near Turkey Creek around 1790. The structure housed several generations of the family, one of the most prominent in 19th-century Knoxville, and is believed to have been used as a hospital during the Civil War, before it passed into the hands of outsiders.

While many mountain dwellings contained only a single room, the McClung House had two—one would have been the kitchen and the other a second living area. When it was built, the cabin was of the type owned by the more well-to-do families in southern Appalachia. An early example of a "dogtrot" house, an architectural type usually found in the Deep South, it is distinguished by a central dogtrot, or breezeway, running through the structure between the two rooms. The origins of the dogtrot are uncertain, but it may have been designed to keep kitchen heat confined to one portion of the house. In the winter it was used for stacking firewood, and in the summer it served as a cool porch extension, where women might sew, shuck corn, or share a bit of gossip.

Many of the furnishings now seen in the McClung House were passed down through the family of John Rice Irwin, the museum's founder; the carved walnut bed, opposite, was made by Irwin's great-grandfather.

Recalling the Appalachian log cabins that were occupied by the same family over many generations, the McClung House is filled with belongings that range in date from the early 1800s to the 1920s. The decorative cherry-and-walnut bed at left was made by Jesse Grant, reportedly a second cousin of Ulysses S. Grant. The pine corner cupboard once stood in the kitchen of John Rice Irwin's grandmother.

MOUNTAIN MUSIC

Tate Elliott of Anderson County, Tennessee, made this square-bodied, five-string banjo in the early 1900s, using scrap poplar and a piece of roofing tin.

This unusual fiddle is the work of Hiram Sharp. In addition to making musical instruments, Sharp also served as a dentist, barber, and undertaker.

This banjo was made from a shipping crate, old signs, and tobacco tins. It belonged to Rufus and Kellie Eledge, who lived near Bearwallow Mountain in the Great Smokies.

This fretless, round-bodied banjo was crafted from curly maple and ground-hog hide; it is thought to be from White Top Mountain in southwestern Virginia.

A Selecto ham can serves as the body for this imaginative banjo, made by Dow Pugh, a well-known woodcarver and folk artist from Putnam County, Tennessee.

Appalachia has long been associated with country music, and to the people of the southern highlands region, country music is synonymous with a string band. While the string band developed around a number of different instruments, the granddaddy of them all is the violin—or fiddle, as it is always called locally. Introduced to Appalachia in the 1700s by early settlers, the fiddle was the first stringed instrument to be brought to the region, and it became the mainstay of rural dances, called "hops" or "frolics."

In the early to mid-1800s, the fiddle was joined by the banjo, or "banjar," whose roots can be traced to the West Indies and Africa. It is thought that an early form of this instrument was introduced in this country by slaves. Tradition has it that a Blue Ridge Mountain boy named Joel Walker Sweeney was the first local resident to adopt the instrument, adding a fifth string, which he made shorter than the other four, for the thumb.

The guitar became part of the string band around 1900. This in-

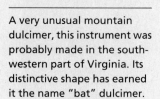

A very unusual mountain dulcimer, this instrument was probably made in the south-western part of Virginia. Its distinctive shape has earned it the name "bat" dulcimer.

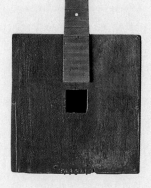

While the square body of this guitar is handcrafted, the neck was taken from an inexpensive factory-made instrument. The guitar probably dates from the 1930s.

This oversize fiddle comes from Jonesboro, Tennessee. The floral designs carved into its body are similar to those found on other instruments made in that area.

Minnie Black of Kentucky grew the gourds that she used in crafting musical instruments. She made this fiddle and bow in celebration of the nation's bicentennial.

strument is thought to have been popularized in the area by men returning from fighting in the Spanish-American War; they had heard it played in the Caribbean, admired it, and brought it home.

One of the stringed instruments found more recently in Appalachia is the dulcimer, which was not widely used until well into the 1900s. The mountain dulcimer probably derives from the 17th-century German *schei-tholt;* both are plucked or played with a bow, in contrast to the hammer dulcimer, which is played with padded hammers.

Before the days of mail order, all of these stringed instruments were invariably made by their Appalachian players. And as it was the custom to improvise with whatever materials were on hand, everything from empty ham cans and cigar boxes to gourds and wildcat hides went into their construction. Two or three homemade instruments could usually be found in even the most isolated households, and the melodies they produced were sure to set feet to tapping and hands to clapping.

General Bunch House

The General Bunch House originally stood in an isolated area of Anderson County, Tennessee, called New River. General Bunch, one of twelve children reared in the two-room home, was just eight years old in 1898 when he helped his father build the house, and could recall using a team of oxen to haul logs down from the mountains for its construction. The dominating feature of the interior is a sandstone fireplace, ingeniously designed as an arch to eliminate the need for an iron support across the top of the opening; iron was especially difficult for backwoods settlers to come by.

Because no Bunch family pieces remained in the house when it was moved to the museum, locally made furnishings were gathered from the area. Filling the rooms, they evoke the atmosphere of an overflowing turn-of-the-century Appalachian household.

In the early 1900s, when General Bunch was growing up in the two-room log house above, a trip to the store meant a twelve-mile hike.

Preserves and everyday utensils are found in the General Bunch House, left; gourds like those on the hearth were cleaned, dried, and used as canisters.

The device mounted over the table in the General Bunch House, right, is a "fly-minder"; when a treadle is operated, the muslin strips swing back and forth, keeping flies away from food.

Irwin's Chapel

Religion played an important role in Appalachian life. A Bible was a valued family possession, and a one-room log chapel or meeting house could be found wherever there was a community large enough to support regular Sunday meetings.

Built around 1840, the little chapel at the Museum of Appalachia originally served the tiny village of Hamburg, North Carolina, just over the Tennessee line, for about a century. The Hamburg congregation eventually moved to a full-size church, and the chapel was bought by a lay preacher named Thomas Tweed for thirty-five dollars and a cowboy hat. The building and its contents were later sold to the museum. Since its original name was unknown, the meeting house was called Irwin's Chapel in honor of John Rice Irwin's grandfather, who was once a preacher in Big Valley, Tennessee.

The interior of Irwin's Chapel is furnished simply, with rustic benches and a pulpit made from one section of an enormous log. The pulpit was intended for the preacher's use; members of the congregation, in turn, stood at one of the lecterns to read from the Scriptures and to lead their neighbors in song.

Hand-split shingles were used to roof Irwin's Chapel, above, and wooden shutters take the place of window glass. The furnishings, right, including the log pulpit and benches and a large rocker crafted of tree branches, are thought to be original to the building.

Historic Old Salem

an early Moravian community in the North Carolina piedmont

Like many other 18th-century immigrants to America, the Moravians—members of a religious society founded in Bohemia in 1457—were pious, law-abiding, and hardworking. Indeed, they were such model citizens that in 1752 they were asked by a British land proprietor to purchase property in the Carolina territory, and a year later the Moravians acquired a tract of approximately one hundred thousand acres in the North Carolina piedmont. It was there, in 1766, that they went on to establish the town of Salem.

Salem was one of the last stops on the Moravians' long journey toward religious freedom. In 1722, persecution had forced these Protestant reformers to flee their homeland in the province of Moravia (in what is now Czechoslovakia) and seek protection in Saxony. There, they adopted many converts, as well as the language and customs that were to give the society its distinctly Germanic character. America, however, represented a permanent refuge, and in 1740 the Moravians started a colony in Bethlehem, Pennsylvania. From Bethlehem, twelve members

Continued

Dated 1768, the earliest extant house in Salem was built in a half-timbered style.

were chosen to establish a foothold in the vast Carolina tract.

Their first settlement was a farming community named Bethabara, where the Moravians lived temporarily while planning their principal town, to be called Salem, from *shalom,* the Hebrew word for peace. Unlike Bethabara, Salem was conceived as a trade and crafts center where individuals would operate their own shops for profit—under Church control.

Indeed, the Moravian Church was the center of life in Salem, overseeing material, civic,

and spiritual affairs. It owned all of the land in town, and stipulated what could be built on it. The Church also founded schools, and structured the social system into groups, called choirs, according to age, sex, and marital status. Families lived in their own houses, although adolescents moved to communal dwellings.

Thriving under this organization, the Moravians created a lively, self-sufficient, and cultured society. Oriented around a central square, the town grew rapidly to include a church, a tavern, schools, tidy homes and shops, the com-

Continued

The houses lining Main Street, above, were originally owned by Moravian families, who also maintained shops in the buildings.

Behind each house in Salem
was a tidy garden where
herbs, flowers, vegetables,
and fruits were grown. The
lilacs, fruit trees, okra, and
Virginia gourdseed corn (an
18th-century variety)
flourishing in the restored
plot at right are all plant
types that were cultivated
by the Moravians.

munal Sisters and Brothers Houses—even a public waterworks. Many of the buildings were constructed with the half-timbered framing methods that the Moravians brought from Europe, giving Salem the look of a German village. Among the structures, however, are early Federal houses, indicating that by the 1800s the Moravians had begun to respond to outside influences.

In the mid-1800s, the effects of the Industrial Revolution were also being felt. Mechanization began to eclipse the handcraftsmanship that was the foundation of the Moravian economy; the choir system dissolved over the next several decades, and the Moravians started to filter into outside society.

By the 1940s, modern Winston-Salem had engulfed the community. Old Salem's original twenty-six-acre core still exists, however, and since the 1950s some sixty structures—most privately owned—have been restored or rebuilt, offering a picture of Salem's development from the 1700s to the mid-1800s. In addition to private homes, restaurants, and stores, are twelve buildings—all original to Salem—that are open to the public under the auspices of Old Salem, Inc., an educational corporation. These include the tavern, the Single Brothers House, shops, and family dwellings. Gardens have been replanted, enhancing the sense that this remarkable Moravian settlement has come back to life.

Native scuppernong grapevines climb over a fence in the garden above, which also features a large pumpkin patch. The tall stakes support masses of pole beans.

101

Moravian Customs

Still active today, the Moravian Church has a long tradition of customs that play an important role in the lives of its members. The followers of Jan Hus, the early-15th-century religious reformer who inspired the Moravian movement, were encouraged by his teachings to break with the Roman Catholic Church and to model their religious rites on the unaffected practices of the early Christians. Thus, holidays, births, confirmations, and other occasions are marked by relatively simple celebrations intended to express fellowship and equality before God.

Some of the customs depicted in the 18th-century engravings at right fell into disuse and have been all but forgotten. Very little is known, for example, about foot washing, or the *pedilavium,* which was practiced on holidays and in connection with Holy Communion in certain 18th-century Moravian communities.

Holy Communion, by contrast, is indeed still celebrated. The Moravians' particular manner of administering the sacrament, a protest against the more ritualized practice of the Catholic Church, developed in the early years of the movement. Rather than approaching an altar individually, the Moravian congregants stand in place to receive consecrated bread and wine in their hands from the minister. When all have

As part of the *pedilavium,* Church deaconesses wash the feet of others; a gesture of humility, the practice was based on an early Christian custom.

Participating in a children's love feast, "menservants" and the "Lord's handmaidens" distribute a simple meal to Moravian boys and girls.

After receiving the bread of Communion from the minister, Moravian "brothers" and "sisters" kneel to partake of the Lord's Supper and to pray.

Moravians gather at a cemetery, called "God's acre," on Easter morning, to honor those who have "fallen asleep in the Lord" and are awaiting resurrection.

been served, the participants kneel to partake together, then sing hymns and pray. The service is concluded with a handshake.

A far more distinctive practice is the Moravian love feast, which began in 1727 in Saxony. For this occasion, Church members gather for a service and a simple meal—often a bun and coffee. This tradition is based on the early Christian practice of joining together to break bread as a symbol of unity with Christ. More than a social function, the love feast is an important expression of fellowship and devotion to God. The service often begins with a prayer, then the meal is passed out by appointed servers while the congregation sings hymns; a closing benediction follows. A love feast might be held on any day on which there is a desire to stress "the oneness and brotherhood" of God's followers, as well as to mark a holy day such as Easter.

The primary Moravian Easter celebration, however, is a dawn service, a custom that originated in 1732 in Saxony. In the early morning darkness, participants march to the church cemetery, which is traditionally known as "God's acre," to the accompaniment of instrumental music (heralding the Resurrection). As the sun rises, the service takes place, with members singing hymns and reciting a confession of faith.

Single Brothers House

The Single Brothers House, above, originally consisted of the half-timbered portion, completed in 1769; the oak supports were used to reinforce brickwork before lime-based mortar was widely available. The all-brick section was added in 1786.

One of the choirs, or groups, that made up Moravian society comprised unmarried men who lived and worked in the Single Brothers House, where living quarters and crafts workshops were located under the same roof. Having completed his elementary education, a boy would join the house when he was fourteen, and stay for at least seven years. While in residence, he was apprenticed to a master craftsman and worked toward the rank of journeyman in a particular trade. At age twenty-one, a single "brother" was free to marry—with the approval of the Church—and could leave the house to go into business for himself, thus relinquishing all involvement with the affairs of the choir. Some brothers, however, remained single and stayed on until the end of their days.

Continued

Single "brothers" ate in the communal dining hall, right, furnished with sawbuck tables; the circa 1776 iron stove is original to the structure.

The pottery, above, features a late-1700s grinding wheel, used to make glazes, as well as a sampling of typical Moravian wares.

The Single Brothers House at Old Salem was originally a half-timbered building begun in 1768 to provide living space and a limited work area for a small number of brethren. When the brick addition was built in 1786 to accommodate the town's expanding population, the new wing was used to house a vespers hall, a kitch-en, a communal dining room, and dormitory-style sleeping quarters, while the old section was devoted to workshops.

The workshops, along with a distillery, a brewery, and a slaughterhouse—all run by the brothers—constituted a manufacturing center unlike anything previously known in the backwoods of

the Carolina territory. Indeed, the Single Brothers House produced much of what was sold in the town, including guns, clocks, barrels, furniture, and woven goods. The setup proved so efficient that even after paying an obligatory share of their incomes to the Church, the brothers were able to realize a profit for their choir.

The eight restored workshops that are run by Old Salem, Inc., are furnished with tools, equipment, and a sampling of the types of goods that the brothers and other artisans made and sold in the town. The pottery, for example, would have produced a wide array of ceramic pieces, including dishware, dolls' heads, and stove tiles, while

Continued

Large compasses, and an antique shaving horse used in shaping barrel staves, are displayed in the cooper's shop, above.

wooden containers were made in the cooperage. Such a workshop would have supplied villagers and local farmers alike with barrels specially designed for both dry and wet goods, as well as with butter churns and gunpowder kegs, and buckets, crates, and tubs for a variety of household uses.

Textile dyeing was another essential trade undertaken by the single brothers. Because Salem did not have a full-time dyer until late in the 1780s, textiles were originally sent to the Bethlehem, Pennsylvania, community for processing, or they were dyed at home. Once the dye shop was in operation, however, patrons could bring in cloth or homespun yarn to be custom-colored; a copper claim check attached to a piece ensured its return to the proper owner.

Although records indicate that red, black, and green colorants were used in the dye shop, 90 percent of the dyers' work involved indigo, a particularly difficult dye to process at home. The yarn and cloth displayed in the shop today, in a variety of shades, including indigo blue, have been treated with the same types of natural vegetal dyes as those used by the Moravians in the 18th century.

As in the years when the single brothers operated the dye shop, yarns today are colored with natural dyes made from berries, barks, flowers, and roots. Lengths of yarn hang to dry near the fire, left, then are twisted and stored neatly on shelves, as above.

MASTER POTTER GOTTFRIED AUST

The production of earthenware was one of the largest industries in Salem, and among the most lucrative. The North Carolina piedmont was rich in excellent clay, and a pottery was conceived as part of the town's original plan. Owned by the Moravian Church, the business, which was started in 1768, was in operation for seventy-five years and turned out wares that were unlike any others made in America during that period.

While a lack of competition in the area helped to ensure financial success, Salem owed much of its early renown as a ceramics center to its first master potter, Gottfried Aust. An innovative artisan who is also remembered for his ill temper, Aust learned his trade among the Moravians in Germany before emigrating to their Bethlehem, Pennsylvania, settlement in 1754. The following year, he moved to the Bethabara, North Carolina, settlement—where he also worked as a potter—then went on to Salem in 1771, remaining there until his death in 1788.

Aust's spacious shop in Salem was located at the northern edge of the town. Following a 1733 Church order that applied to all enterprises in the community, it was identified by a trade sign: the master potter's was an elaborately decorated ceramic plate measuring over twenty-one inches in diameter. Aust's custom-

ers, who included townsfolk as well as outsiders from near and far, evidently had no trouble finding him, as records indicate that his ceramic wares sold out almost as soon as they were produced.

Aust created a wide range of utilitarian and decorative pieces, repre-

Glazed to imitate English Whieldon ware, the ceramic tiles on this c. 1775 stove typify those made by Aust.

sented by the sampling of tile molds and ceramic works shown opposite—all of which are attributed to the master potter. Among the common household goods he made were simple bowls, plates, pots, jugs, and lamps, as well as stove tiles and tobacco pipes. Such pieces were generally fired with a lead glaze—either clear, or colored brown or green—to

seal the porous clay. They featured little ornament other than sponging or a simple molded motif, such as the "Patera Shell" or "Spiral Flower" patterns found on the tiles.

It was on the large plates and other fancy pieces traditionally reserved for display that Aust's genius for decoration was clearly demonstrated. Using a slip cup, the potter might trail wavy lines, circles, or scallops around the edge of a piece, then add a lively spray of flowers with fernlike leaves. The elaborate scrollwork that he also created with slip recalls the ornate calligraphy of the illuminated fraktur, which were popular at the time.

While Aust often adapted traditional Germanic motifs, such as flowers, he was also willing to experiment with designs and techniques. The craftsman was especially interested in English pottery forms and decoration, such as the mottled veining characteristic of Whieldon ware. With the help of an itinerant English potter named William Ellis, who visited Salem in 1773, Aust also learned to craft Queen's ware, a type of creamware popularized in England by Josiah Wedgwood in the 1760s. Aust experimented with Queen's ware, but never produced it on a large scale. Instead, his work, as well as that of other Salem potters, always remained closely tied to the Germanic craft heritage of central Europe.

Aust's 1773 red ceramic shop sign, decorated in white and green slip

Stove tile with the "Spiral Flower" pattern; Salem, c. 1771-1788

Display plate with polychrome decoration; Salem, c. 1771-1788

Simple teapot with brown glaze; Bethabara, c. 1755-1771

Display plate with floral design; Salem, c. 1771-1788

Mold used for making a stove tile in the "Patera Shell" pattern

Mold for a tile designed to complement the "Patera Shell" pattern

Display plate with typical floral decoration; Salem, c. 1771-1788

Display plate with abstract border design; Salem, c. 1771-1788

Display plate with Germanic tulip decoration; Salem, c. 1771-1788

Betty lamp with brown glaze; Bethabara, c. 1755-1771

"Patera Shell" tile glazed to imitate marble veining; Salem, c. 1771-1788

Salem Tavern

A clean, comfortable rest stop for travelers, Salem Tavern was built in 1784 on the foundation of an earlier inn that had been destroyed by fire. The tavern was known throughout the region for its hospitality; even George Washington, a guest in 1791, was impressed. However, this gathering place also proved attractive to the Moravian townspeople, whom the Church feared would indulge to excess and fall under the influence of outsiders. After the board of overseers, responsible for managing town affairs, noted that a "party of Brothers has had a gay time at the tavern," the innkeeper was reminded to restrict entrance to "traveling strangers only."

Those who did enter met with a choice of

Continued

Between 1772 and 1850, the Moravian Church operated a tavern in Salem, catering to the many outsiders who came to the town to purchase goods and services. The 1784 tavern above was designed in the Germanic tradition, with no windows on the first floor of the street façade—useful for discouraging the Moravian townsfolk from looking in.

Travelers could expect a hearty meal—or a game of chess—in the public room, left. Food was served on pewter and pottery wares at communal tables.

113

In the Gentlemen's Room, right, travelers could order meals at any time of day— and dined at tables set with fine tableware, such as the 18th-century English cream-ware plates and stemmed glasses shown here. Gin, brandy, rum, wine, and beer, along with such mixed drinks as grogs and toddies, would have been dispensed from the small bar.

facilities. Common folk ate in the main public room, where the "ordinary" (a dinner served at set times) was eaten at communal tables. Travelers of a "better sort," who could afford to order food when they wanted it, were entertained in the more elegant Gentlemen's Room. The food, prepared by the innkeeper's wife, earned an excellent reputation for the tavern, which returned a high profit for the Church.

After weary travelers had dined, they could retire to the communal and private bedrooms on the second floor. Eighteenth-century records indicate that while there were generally fewer than ten beds available at the inn, up to sixty individuals could be accommodated per .night; the barn supplied extra space for overnight guests.

The bedroom above was used by an aide to George Washington during the president's 1791 visit to Salem.

115

The spacious kitchen, right, was the largest in Salem in the 18th century. Meals were cooked at the two hearths; the fireplace on the left is also equipped with a bake oven. Beef fat rendered in the cooking process would have been used to make candles like those hanging from the circa 1800 candle wheel in the foreground.

John Vogler House

John Vogler, who commissioned the 1819 house above, was the first Moravian in Salem to break with tradition by building a home in the English-inspired Federal style. The door hood is painted with a clock face, Vogler's trade sign.

One of the most prominent and prosperous citizens in 19th-century Salem was John Vogler, an accomplished and versatile craftsman. Coming to Salem at age nineteen, young Vogler apprenticed under his uncle, a gunsmith, and learned the rudiments of woodworking and smithing. He began his career as a silversmith, but subsequently tried his hand at selling optical equipment, making jewelry, and cutting silhouettes, as well as repairing timepieces, a profession considered to be particularly prestigious. As the craftsman, who lived to be ninety-seven, said, "Industry was never a burden to me and my hands could generally perform what the mind dictated."

The profits of that "industry" went into building his stately brick house, which Vogler erected in 1819 next to the community store—a highly

Continued

Family pieces in the parlor, right, include a French clock, a leather-backed rocker, and the circa 1830 portraits of the Voglers.

Even ordinary hardware was finely crafted by the Moravians, who believed that beauty was appreciated by God. The 1786 engraved brass "elbow" latch above not only shows exquisite workmanship, but also features an ingenious design: the elongated iron handle can be depressed with an elbow if one's hands are full.

desirable location for a craftsman, who customarily sold his wares out of a first-floor shop. Impressed by the Federal town houses he saw while on frequent business trips to Philadelphia, Vogler commissioned a residence in the same style. With its trim, symmetrical design, the building was the first English-inspired Federal-style house in Salem; Germanic architecture had previously been the rule.

The interior, as refined as the exterior, has now been restored, and shows that the Vogler family—which by 1825 included a son, Elias, and two daughters, Lisetta and Louisa Lauretta—lived in considerable comfort. The eight rooms are decorated as they might have been in the 1830s, with fancy painted woodwork, wallpapers, fine furniture, and such imported goods as English china. The house also features a tiled stove like the one the Voglers would have used. These efficient heating devices were common in central Europe, and the Moravians continued to produce and use them in America.

Continued

The Neoclassical, paw-footed tile stove in the dining room, above, was crafted by the Salem potter Heinrich Schaffner around 1840. In the kitchen, right, an early-19th-century "Cooks Favourite" stove replaces the original; the Voglers probably had the first cast-iron stove in Salem.

The master bedroom, right, is dominated by the Voglers' circa 1820 tester bed, a formal piece that features ebonized ball feet, a stipple-painted cornice, and classical urn finials (a Moravian trademark). Silhouettes of the couple's three children are displayed beside the window; an accomplished silhouette artist, Vogler cut these portraits himself.

Many of the furnishings, donated by Vogler's descendants for the restoration, are original to the house. The showpiece of the master bedroom (preceding overleaf), for example, is the elegant, circa 1820 curly-maple tester bed that the Voglers bought soon after their marriage. The room also features Mrs. Vogler's maple sewing table, her rocking chair, and the cradle in which her infants slept.

Other furnishings in the house are known to have been used or crafted in Salem. The children's bedrooms, left and above, for instance, feature Moravian-made beds. Also on display is an array of 19th-century toys, of the type enjoyed by Salem's young folk. The Moravians cherished their children, called "the Lord's delight" by a leading Church figure, and believed that toys such as tea sets, building blocks, and rocking horses were not frivolous, but helped to develop a child's mind and body.

The chamber at left is presented as the room shared by the two Vogler girls; the circa 1825 tester bed was made by the same Salem joiner who crafted their parents' bed. The rocking horse and blocks in the boy's room, above, date to the 1800s, and typify toys used by Moravian children.

Hancock Shaker Village

*the Shaker way
of life recalled in the
Berkshire Hills*

In the 1780s, Mother Ann Lee—the spiritual leader of the Shakers—who had left her native England for America in 1774, traveled through the Northeast promoting her religious beliefs: separation from "the world," communal living, and celibacy. Her words fell on receptive ears among several western Massachusetts families, who in 1790 founded a settlement in the town of Hancock; here new members of the sect, formally known as the United Society of Believers in Christ's Second Appearing, could live according to Shaker principles.

The third Shaker village to be established in America—by 1840 there would be eighteen such communities—the settlement steadily attracted converts and grew rapidly. During its peak years in the 1830s, it covered some two thousand acres and boasted three sawmills, a ten-acre "physic" garden of medicinal herbs, an impressive round stone barn, a forty-five-room brick dwelling house, a meeting house, numerous farm outbuildings,

Continued

The Brick Dwelling House was once the focal point of this Shaker community.

workshops, a woolen mill, and 250 residents. Segregated by sex, each Believer was a member of a "family" consisting of fifty to one hundred "brothers" or "sisters." The families, in turn, were governed by "elders" and "eldresses," who saw to the spiritual needs of the members, and by "deacons" and "deaconesses," who managed the family workload. As in all mid-19th-century Shaker communities, life was regulated by "Millennial Laws," which specified everything from proper personal behavior and dress to room furnishings and paint colors. Days were punctuated by the sounds of bells that determined when members woke up, ate meals, worshiped, worked, and went to sleep. Yet, despite its regimented nature, life was not unpleasant for these warm, humorous people, who also enjoyed such diversions as picnics, sleigh rides, and singing.

Above all, the community was perhaps best characterized by its efficient ways. In fact, when it came to work, which was deemed a form of worship, the Shakers were remarkably resourceful in easing the burden of their tasks. They were great inventors, and their buildings incorporated many conveniences, such as removable window sashes (for easy cleaning) and dumb-

waiters. The massive, three-level round dairy barn at Hancock, which held some fifty cows, is particularly notable for its laborsaving design. Up to ten wagons could drive around the top area. From there, hay was dumped into a central mow that was ringed by stalls; trap doors allowed manure to be swept into the basement.

The remarkable stone dairy barn is just one of many Shaker structures that now make up the museum known as Hancock Shaker Village, which was started by a group of local citizens who purchased a thousand acres of the property in 1960. At that time, the village was largely derelict, and only three Shaker sisters remained.

After years of research and restoration, however, much now appears as it once did. Rooms are filled with plain, graceful furniture that expresses the Shaker belief in simplicity. Workshops are outfitted with the Shaker-made tools and equipment originally used in cottage industries such as broom making, basketweaving, and seed packaging. Both the buildings and their contents provide insight into a society of remarkably open-minded people who practiced tolerance, believed in equality of the sexes and races, and while living simply, welcomed progress.

Fronting the massive 1826 round stone barn, above, are tidy plots planted with medicinal herbs. These represent only a sampling of the many varieties cultivated by the Hancock Shakers, whose herb garden originally covered ten acres.

The Meeting House

The plain appearance of the Meeting House, above, reflects the Shaker belief that religion was centered in individuals rather than in their place of worship.

The circa 1792 Meeting House was brought to the village from a Shaker community in Shirley, Massachusetts, to replace one that was taken down in 1938. Framed by the same Shaker builder who erected the original Hancock meeting house, it is also identical in design. There are no pulpit, altar, or pews, as the Shakers did not require them for their methods of worship. Instead, members used portable benches, which could be moved out of the way to accommodate the dancing that was part of a service; benches along the walls were for the elderly and visitors.

As specified by the Millennial Laws, the interior woodwork, right, is painted "a blueish shade."

SHAKER "LABORING"

Like many aspects of Shaker life, the sect's manner of worship did not conform to mainstream thinking. Although Shakers were Christians and read the King James Bible —as did many other religious groups in 18th- and 19th-century New England—there were no clergy or masses in Shaker services. Moreover, the Believers indulged in a practice on

"Humility"

the Sabbath—and in their meeting houses—that was forbidden by many other denominations: they danced.

Shaker dancing, or "laboring," grew out of the peculiar movement that was part of the services held in the early years of the society. Worshipers customarily meditated in silence during their Sabbath meetings, but might gesticulate, twitch, whirl, stamp, or fall on impulse. Such movement, which also included the shaking that gave the sect its name, was considered to be a manifestation

of the Spirit. Among the other religious groups that practiced such behavior were the Quakers, from whom the Shakers stemmed.

By the 1800s, Shaker services had become more organized, evolving into standardized pattern dances as movement became less spontaneous. After a period of meditation, a member might say, "Brethren and sisters, let us labor," and everyone would join in a ritualized, symbolic dance to the accompaniment of a song. "Laboring" referred to the effort believed necessary to become receptive to spiritual influence.

Participants might march in straight ranks, which signified the travel of the soul to heaven, or shuffle around in a ring, meant to symbolize never-ending fellowship. Individual postures and gestures were also used to convey the meaning of a dance and its accompanying song. One move-

"Warring Song"

"Coming of Inspiration"

ment involved a low bow, with arms back, as a sign of humility. In another posture, part of the "Warring Song," arms were crossed to ward off evil.

To accommodate the Shaker style of worship, meeting houses were designed with a large, open room. Men and women filed in through separate entrances and were often joined by visitors. Outsiders, who did not participate, usually came to watch the dancing out of sheer curiosity. Yet the Shakers nevertheless encouraged "the world's people" to attend their services in the hopes of gaining converts and publicizing their community. Some observers were favorably impressed, but others, like Ralph Waldo Emerson, were definitely not: "Senseless jumping," scoffed the writer after visiting a Shaker meeting in the 1820s.

Shakers in the New Lebanon, New York, community are shown dancing,
or "laboring," above; men and women danced in separate groups.

The Shakers above, at the Watervliet, New York, settlement, are
performing a "wheel" dance as elderly members of the sect look on.

The Brick Dwelling House

The six-level Brick Dwelling House, which cost the remarkable sum of eight thousand dollars when it was built in 1830-1831, is evidence of the prosperity the Hancock Shakers then enjoyed. Housing forty-six brethren and forty-eight sisters—separated by a central hallway and their common vow of celibacy—the forty-five-room residence functioned as the heart of community life; here sect members ate, slept, and worshiped at weekday meetings.

Characteristically, the dwelling house was well organized, with rooms allocated to specific purposes. In the basement were storage rooms, as well as a large kitchen equipped with stone sinks, running water, bake ovens, and "arch kettles," unique built-in steam cookers. The first floor featured common rooms, including a meeting room used for evening services and a dining room. On the second and third floors were twenty sleeping, or "retiring," rooms, each shared by four to five members of the sect. Separate entryways led to the brothers' section, on the east side of the building, and to the sisters' rooms, on the west.

Today only three rooms are presented as retiring rooms; the others are used to interpret

Continued

Believing light to be a gift from God, the Shakers built the Brick Dwelling House with ninety-five windows. Furnishings like the chairs, beds, and rug in the retiring room at right were Shaker-made.

The room at left is set up for "union meetings," which took place in one of the retiring rooms. Here, several of the brethren and sisters would gather—their chairs always spaced "at least five feet" apart—to quietly socialize and sing hymns. Such meetings were believed to satisfy the need for "correspondence" between men and women, who were separated during most of the day.

The cupboard above holds Shaker-made boxes. The box labeled "Shaker Anodyne" once contained valerian, an herb used as a sedative and recommended for neuralgia and nervousness.

Shaker activities that originally took place elsewhere. The room above and at right, for example, is set up as a pharmacy, where the Shakers would have prepared a range of tinctures, extracts, pills, and balms.

Such remedies were generally administered to patients by certain sect members who served as healers. These individuals would have worked in an infirmary, or "nurse shop," represented by the display (overleaf). This sickroom, also on view in the dwelling house, is equipped with Shaker-made crutches, an adjustable bed, and cradles built especially for adults.

At right, mortars and pestles, vials, and beakers, all used by the Shakers to make pharmaceuticals from plants, are exhibited in the pharmacy.

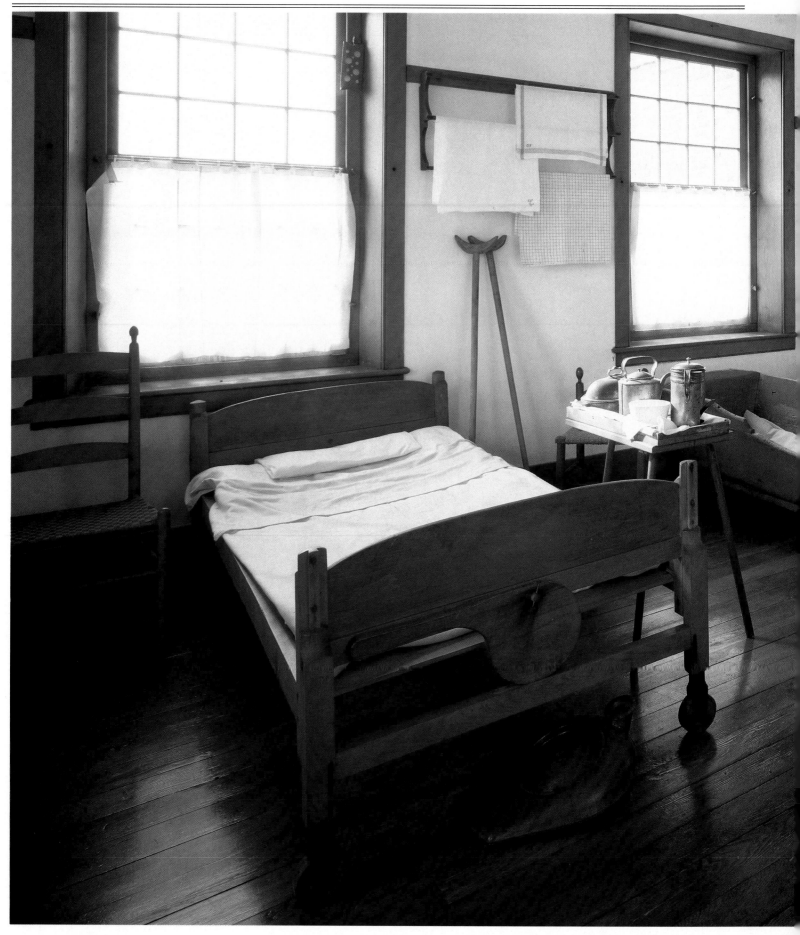

A sickroom like the one at left would originally have been located in a separate "nurse shop," used for the care of the infirm and the elderly; Hancock had two such facilities, one for the brethren and one for the sisters. The cradles for adults were considered therapeutic, as the rocking motion was soothing and helped prevent bedsores.

Laundry and Machine Shop

Deep red was deemed the proper color for Shaker service buildings. The structure above housed a laundry and a machine shop at the Hancock community.

Begun in 1790, the service building above originally housed a machine shop, which was operated by the Shaker brethren, and a laundry, run by the sisters. Both facilities were served by water piped in from a nearby pond to a basement water wheel.

Typically, the laundry was designed for maximum efficiency. Clothes and linens were cleaned in a first-floor washroom, then hoisted to a drying area located on an upper story to take advantage of the rising heat. Dry laundry was dropped down a chute to the ironing room, right, where a Shaker-made stove heated dozens of irons at a time.

Today, the building also houses an exhibit (overleaf) devoted to the Shaker seed business; the Shakers were the first people in America to package garden seeds commercially.

Clothes were sorted, then pressed on counters in the ironing room, right, six days a week.

Known for their high quality,
Shaker goods were in
demand among outsiders; in
1850, for example, more
than seven thousand dollars
worth of seeds were sold to
"the world." In a room like
the one at right, the sisters
would have dried herbs and
flowers, and prepared vegetables, to extract the seeds.
These were then carefully
sorted, and packaged in
paper envelopes that were
designed, produced, and
printed in village
workshops.

El Rancho de las Golondrinas

*an outdoor history museum
of early settlement in
New Mexico*

El Rancho de las Golondrinas, the Ranch of the Swallows, in La Cienega, New Mexico, takes its name from the flocks of birds that migrate to this valley near Santa Fe at the same time each spring. The name has endured for centuries, along with the ranch itself, now a two-hundred-acre outdoor museum set amid rolling hills that are fragrant with sagebrush and junipers.

The museum, which recalls the history of the area's settlement—both as a Spanish colony and, after 1846, as a United States territory—was started by Leonora Curtin and Y. A. Paloheimo, a couple who moved to the property in 1946. At the time, the ranch had been in the Curtin family for years, but only a few of the old structures existed, including the remains of two ranch houses. Because the couple were intrigued by the early methods of stone and adobe construction these buildings represented, they began restoring crumbling walls and collapsing

Continued

The chapel in the restored placita compound, opposite, retains its original stone walls.

The doorway above is the only entry into the fortified placita *compound. The large wooden gates could be swung open to admit wagons and animals; smaller doors within the gates accommodated human traffic.*

roofs. They also began to look for other early structures they could move to the ranch, and started assembling a collection of period furnishings the settlers might have owned. As work progressed, the idea for a museum slowly developed; that museum eventually opened in 1972. Formally known as Old Cienega Village Museum at El Rancho de las Golondrinas, it incorporates early restored and reconstructed buildings as well as reproductions, and consists of three major components: the 18th-century *placita* house, the early 1800s Baca residence, and the Sierra Village, a separate group of buildings in the nearby hills.

The oldest part of the museum is the restored *placita* house, actually a complex of interconnected dwellings, workrooms, storage areas, and a chapel, all opening onto a central *placita*, or

courtyard. Dating to about 1710, this expansive compound was built by one of the first Spanish colonial owners of the ranch, and would have originally housed about fifty members of an extended family. As fortification against Comanche attacks, the solid enclosing wall incorporated a watchtower, where a sentinel would be posted.

Adjacent to the *placita* house is the Baca House, named for the family of Spanish colonial settlers who purchased the property in the 1700s and owned it for nearly two hundred years. The house standing today, part of a complex that once included several detached outbuildings arranged around a courtyard, was built by a member of the Baca family in the early 1800s. By that time, settlers no longer felt the threat of Indian attacks, and the house, sheds, and other build-

Continued

The tower, or torreón, *left, was built into the wall surrounding the circa 1710* placita *compound by order of the king of Spain. During Spanish settlement, three such towers were erected in the La Cienega valley to help defend the colony against attack.*

ings were surrounded by a simple fence rather than by the type of defensive wall that characterizes the *placita* house.

Set in the hills just above the *placita* compound and the Baca House is the third part of the museum, the Sierra Village. The village consists of early dwellings, barns, slave quarters, and a small chapel, which were moved to the ranch property, and is intended to suggest the way settlers lived in the mountains of New Mexico. Still other 18th- and 19th-century buildings, including a blacksmith shop, a gristmill, a wheelwright's shop, a winery, and a *morada*, or religious meeting house, are scattered across the landscape nearby. Completing the museum setting, these structures would also have been part of a typical New Mexico settlement.

Set on a rocky outcropping, the building at left is a reproduction of a 1700s religious meeting house in Abiquiu, New Mexico. In Spanish it is called a morada, or "dwelling place" (for the spirit).

Religion was an extremely important force in Spanish colonial outposts, and family chapels like the one above, at the museum's Sierra Village, were common. A little altar inside is dedicated to San Isidro, the patron saint of farmers.

The Placita House

Established fifteen miles south of Santa Fe, El Rancho de las Golondrinas was situated on the Camino Real, or the Royal Road, which linked the Spanish colonial capitals of Mexico City and Santa Fe. For the soldiers and merchants who traveled between the two cities, the thirteen-hundred-mile journey meant months on the road. The ranch house was an important stopping place for these passersby, as well as a home to the extended family of Spanish settlers who lived on the property.

Accommodations were simple in this residence, built around 1710 and now known as the *placita* house: visitors might sleep in the *placita* (or courtyard) itself, or, if there was space, in one of the interconnected dwellings opening onto it. The dwellings were typically single rooms where the ranchers and their families cooked and slept. The walls were made of adobe bricks finished with adobe plaster. Floors were of hard-packed dirt, which might be sealed with animal blood to minimize dust. Pine beams, or *vigas*, supported ceilings typically covered with stripped tree branches laid side by side.

Some of the one-room dwellings also featured shepherds' fireplaces, named for the shepherds who, as tradition has it, came in from the mountains on cold nights to sleep on the warm loft beds built atop the cooking areas. The actual fireplace was used for heating as well as for cooking, which was done at ground level. Bread-baking, however, took place outdoors in the *placita,* where beehive-shaped adobe ovens were maintained for communal family use.

The walled **placita** *compound, above, houses numerous one-room dwellings like that at left. The simple, all-purpose room contains a shepherd's fireplace, with a bed on top, and a hanging cradle. The clay cooking pots would have been acquired from neighboring Pueblo tribes.*

Some rooms in the placita
compound might have been
used by travelers making
their way between Mexico
City and Santa Fe along the
Camino Real. In the room
at right, guests would have
slept on the floor, but there
also would have been cer-
tain amenities; among those
shown here are a private
altar and a wooden chandelier, which can be lowered
with a rope to make candle
lighting easier.

Few houses in the isolated southwestern settlements would have been without an altar dedicated to a particular saint. A santo, or image of a saint, like the circa 1840 Holy Child of Atocha, above, might be made by a santero—a craftsman who specialized in such images—or by family members.

New Mexican Santeros

Known as *santos,* the religious folk-art pieces at right are representative of the primitive yet extremely expressive devotional works that were made for village churches and homes in late-18th- and early-19th-century northern New Mexico.

The craftsmen, or *santeros,* who produced such paintings (*retablos*) and carvings (*bultos*) often based their work on the flamboyant yet naturalistic baroque art then prevalent in the urban centers of Europe and Mexico. *Santos,* however, still had the naive character of a folk art produced in isolated mountain villages. Since most of the *santeros* did not have the benefit of formal training, perspective was awkwardly handled and the features of the saints and other holy personages who were customarily portrayed were simplified. As a result, the New Mexican pieces have a kind of abstracted, divine quality that sets them apart from the decidedly more humanized and worldly renderings that distinguished baroque art. In turn, the *santos* seem especially appropriate expressions of the simple piety and devotion that characterized rural religious life.

While some *santeros*—few of whom are known by name—worked individually, they often collaborated on pieces. One such man is the anonymous "Laguna" *santero,* so named for his major extant work, the altar screen in the church at the Laguna Pueblo. Active from around 1796 to 1808, this artist is known to have created numerous altar screens and panel paintings on his own, but he also directed a *taller,* or workshop, that employed a variety of artisans, including painters, woodcarvers, and carpenters. The workshop produced altar screens, panel and hide paintings, gessoed relief panels, and decorative niches.

Another *santero* who worked both by himself and in a *taller* was José Rafael Aragón, known for the devotional paintings, altar screens, and sculptures he produced between 1820 and 1862. Compared to the majority of *santeros,* Aragón came from a cosmopolitan background. For many years, he lived in Santa Fe, which was then the cultural capital of New Mexico, and may have studied art there. This would account for his comparatively sophisticated style, marked by a strong sense of color and line.

An artist whose colorful style is often compared to that of José Rafael Aragón is the "Santo Nino" *santero,* a woodcarver who also worked in the mid-19th century. His small sculptures, with their highly expressive faces, are idealized versions of human figures. Similarly, the works of two other anonymous *santeros* of the period are notable for their particular character: the *santos* of the "A. J." *santero* have a distinctive spontaneity, and those of the "Truchas Master" are especially mystical, with a flat, linear quality that suggests the influence of imported engravings and woodcut prints.

Our Lady of Guadalupe, paint on wood panel; "Truchas Master," 1780-1840

Saint Achatius, bulto with painted background; José Rafael Aragón, 1820-1862

Saint Joseph, painted wood *bulto;*
"Santo Nino" *santero,* 1830-1860

The Flight into Egypt, tempera and gesso on wood; José Rafael Aragón, c. 1850

Saint Joseph, painted wood *bulto;*
José Rafael Aragón, 1820-1862

Saint Joseph, paint and gesso on wood
panel; "A. J." *santero,* 1820s

Saint John Nepomuk, paint on pine
panel; "Laguna" *santero,* 1796-1808

Baca House

In the early 1800s, a descendant of Manuel Baca, the earliest owner of El Rancho de las Golondrinas who is known by name, built an adobe house adjacent to the *placita* compound. In contrast to the spare, single-room dwellings of that earlier complex, the house, above, had two spacious rooms lit by large windows, and several pieces of serviceable handmade wooden furniture.

The kitchen, at right, shows some of the improvements that were in evidence by the 1800s. The cooking area features a bell-shaped fireplace, recessed into a wall, where pots were set over the fire. A second adobe fireplace with a circular opening served as an oven. The flat top could be used to warm food, and might double as a work surface for preparing meals. Convenient to the oven was a cabinet, or *alacena,* which, built into the insulating adobe wall, helped to keep foods cool; for true cold storage, however, perishables were customarily hung in the well in the courtyard just outside the house.

Instead of being set low, as on a shepherd's fireplace, the loft bed over this cooking area is close to the ceiling, allowing room to stand underneath. The posts protruding from the bed frame would have been used for hanging dried herbs, corn, chilies, and other staples that might be wanted close at hand. At the opposite end of the kitchen (overleaf), a simple table and benches placed by a window would have provided extra work space, as well as a place for dining.

The Baca House, above, was one of the first buildings to be restored on the ranch. In the early 1800s
when the house was built, the ranch supported about fifty to seventy-five members of an extended
family, who worked the fields, tended sheep, and kept the buildings in good repair.

Among the cooking imple-
ments adopted by Spanish
colonial settlers from Indi-
ans who lived in the area
were grinding stones like
those in the kitchen of the
Baca House, left. By the
early 1800s, metal uten-
sils would also have
been available.

At right, plaster on a wall of the Baca House kitchen has been chipped away to reveal the unusual bricks that were used to build the house. These were hand-cut directly from clay found in nearby marshes; adobe bricks were more typically made from molds.

The General Store

In many ways, large ranches such as El Rancho de las Golondrinas had to function like small villages, since these isolated homesteads were often at least a day's journey from the nearest town. The most convenient solution to the problem was to open a general store on the ranch itself. Offering goods for barter or for cash, the store could provide for basic day-to-day needs. It also generated extra income for the ranch when travelers stopped in to buy food and supplies for their long journeys, or to purchase the saddles, tinware, and woven textiles that were made on the property.

The merchandise now displayed in the General Store at El Rancho de las Golondrinas includes local produce, such as strings of chilies, that would have been found there in early years, but most items are from the late 1800s—when the railroad had reached Santa Fe. The trains made it possible for all manner of "Anglo" goods sent from the East, including bolts of cotton fabric and tins of biscuits, to reach the Southwest.

Among the most welcome of the new products were those made of iron. Because iron was not found in the New Mexico territory, it was extremely desirable, and was much in demand for the manufacture of tools, hardware, wagon wheels, and horseshoes. At the time of early colonial settlement in the Southwest, iron and iron products had to be brought in by wagon, but the arrival of the railroad in 1879 increased their availability.

At the General Store, above and right, ranch inhabitants and travelers alike might buy items imported from the East, including washboards and flatirons, as well as goods that came from the ranch itself, such as hand-spun wool yarn. Daily necessities like grains and eggs were also available.

Mora House

The Sierra Village at El Rancho de las Golondrinas is representative of settlements found in the higher reaches of northern New Mexico in the mid- to late 19th century. The Mora House, named for its original owners, is the largest residence in the village and is a classic example of a mountain farmhouse of the period.

As trees were abundant in the mountains, wood was freely used for the floors, doors, moldings, and ceilings, as well as for the board-and-batten roof. The roof itself is pitched rather than flat—an effective design for shedding the heavy snows that fall in the higher altitudes of New Mexico. The wide porch running along the front of the house would have provided a dry place for storage, as well as a pleasant spot for a family to rest after a long day of farming.

Although the rooms were sparsely furnished, care was taken to dress them up with color. Decorative borders might be applied to the adobe walls, using sheep's wool that had been dipped in mud. The bright handmade furniture was carved or painted with designs that often derived from weaving patterns, or it was simply finished with whatever color of paint was on hand. Floor coverings and other textiles, customarily woven by both men and women, were made with wool from the sheep that were typically raised on the mountain farms.

The pitched roof on the 19th-century Mora House, above, is a sign of Anglo-American influence on southwestern architecture, as are the paneled doors and molded door frames inside, left. Virtually all of the furnishings in such a mountain farmhouse would have been made on the premises.

Grandmother's House

Families in Spanish colonial mountain settlements were close-knit. Older generations, who participated in work on the farm for as long as possible, were accorded great respect, and stayed close to their relatives. A widowed grandmother would not have lived alone but with one or two of her grandchildren, sharing a little house—efficiently set up for cooking and sleeping—similar to the rustic Grandmother's House at the Sierra Village.

Such a living arrangement was quite practical. The children provided companionship and could help their grandmothers with gardening and other strenuous tasks. Meanwhile, the younger folk would be taught useful skills such as cooking, spinning, and weaving, and were a ready audience for the family stories and lore passed on by their elders.

The little log Grandmother's House, above, features a pitched roof, which accommodates loft space underneath. A ladder was often left atop the roof for easy access when repairs were needed.

At left, the simple furnishings in the one-room Grandmother's House include a spool bed and a metal washstand set beside it.

The Primitive House

Although the Primitive House, above, was built in the 19th century, its heavy door is a salvaged piece from an earlier structure and is thought to have been made around 1700.

The Primitive House, a two-room log cabin at the Sierra Village, was built in the 19th century, but in the flat-roofed style of earlier structures. With its hard-packed dirt floor, roughly hewn doors and woodwork, and extremely simple furnishings, the house is about as rustic as a dwelling can be. Yet at the same time, it demonstrates that a little cabin in the mountains, designed as a basic shelter, could be made quite homey.

The house—which has only a kitchen and an all-purpose room for living and sleeping—might easily have been lived in by several members of a family. The bed in the living area was designed to fold up against the wall to save space when it was not in use. The sheepskins and goatskins that served as rugs and seat covers provided warmth and a bit of comfort. For color, the walls were typically stenciled using *tierra amarilla,* or yellow earth, mixed with water.

In the Primitive House, sheepskins tied to the underside of the folding bed, left, are covered with texts listing the names of early settlers in northern New Mexico. Also included is a poem written in their honor.

Museum Information

For specific information about hours, programs, and events, you can contact
the museums in this book at the following addresses and telephone numbers.

Historic Deerfield, Inc.
P.O. Box 321
Deerfield, MA 01342
(413) 774-5581

The Museum of Appalachia
P.O. Box 359
Norris, TN 37828
(615) 494-7680

Hancock Shaker Village
P.O. Box 898
Pittsfield, MA 01202
(413) 443-0188

Genesee Country Museum
P.O. Box 1819
Rochester, NY 14603
(716) 325-1776

Historic Old Salem
P.O. Box F, Salem Station
Winston-Salem, NC 27108
(919) 721-7300

El Rancho de las Golondrinas
Route 14, P.O. Box 214
Santa Fe, NM 87505
(505) 471-2261

Museum and Photography Credits

Cover: courtesy of the Museum of Appalachia, Norris, TN/Steven Mays. Frontispiece: courtesy of Genesee Country Museum, Mumford, NY/George Ross. Page 8: courtesy of Historic Deerfield, Inc., Deerfield, MA/George Ross. Pages 10-11: courtesy of Historic Deerfield, Inc./Paul Rocheleau. Pages 12-27: courtesy of Historic Deerfield, Inc./George Ross. Page 28: (top) courtesy of the Connecticut Historical Society, Hartford, CT/Robert J. Bitondi; (bottom) courtesy of the American Antiquarian Society, Worcester, MA. Page 29: (clockwise from top left) courtesy of the American Antiquarian Society; the Toledo Museum of Art, Toledo, OH; the Historical Society of York County, York, PA; Jon Elliott; the Corcoran Gallery of Art, Washington, D.C. Pages 30-37: courtesy of Historic Deerfield, Inc./George Ross. Page 39: Steven Mays. Pages 40-45: courtesy of Genesee Country Museum/George Ross. Pages 46-47: (inset photos) Steven Mays; (black-and-white photos) courtesy of the Cobblestone Society Collections, Albion, NY/Gerda Peterich. Pages 48-65: (except 50 left and 56 left) courtesy of Genesee Country Museum/George Ross; (50 left) David Arky; (56 left) courtesy of David A. Schorsch, Inc., NYC. Page 66: "The Quack's Song" from the William H. Helfand Collection/Rob Whitcomb. Page 67: Steven Mays. Pages 68-73: courtesy of Genesee Country Museum/George Ross. Pages 74-81: courtesy of the Museum of Appalachia/Steven Mays. Page 82: "Heritage" by James Still from *The Wolfpen Poems*. Copyright © 1986 Berea College Press, Berea, KY. Reprinted by permission of the author. Pages 82-83: (except 83 far right) photos courtesy of the Museum of Appalachia; (83 far right) picnickers photo courtesy of the Alice Lloyd College Photographic Archives, Alice Lloyd College, Pippa Passes, KY. Pages 84-95: courtesy of the Museum of Appalachia/Steven Mays. Pages 96-101: courtesy of Historic Old Salem, Winston-Salem, NC/Steven Mays. Pages 102-103: courtesy of Historic Old Salem. Pages 104-109: courtesy of Historic Old Salem/Steven Mays. Pages 110-111: courtesy of Historic Old Salem. Pages 112-125: courtesy of Historic Old Salem/Steven Mays. Pages 126-131: courtesy of Hancock Shaker Village, Pittsfield, MA/George Ross. Page 132: courtesy of the Fruitlands Museum, Harvard, MA. Page 133: courtesy of the Shaker Museum, Old Chatham, NY. Pages 134-135: courtesy of Hancock Shaker Village/George Ross. Pages 136-137: courtesy of Hancock Shaker Village/Michael Freeman. Pages 138-139: courtesy of Hancock Shaker Village/George Ross. Pages 140-141: courtesy of Hancock Shaker Village/Michael Freeman. Pages 142-145: courtesy of Hancock Shaker Village/George Ross. Pages 146-155: (except 155 right) courtesy of El Rancho de las Golondrinas, Santa Fe, NM/Steven Mays; (155 right) courtesy of the Taylor Museum of the Colorado Springs Fine Arts Center, Colorado Springs, CO. Pages 156-157: (except 157 top row, second from right) courtesy of the Taylor Museum of the Colorado Springs Fine Arts Center; (157 top row, second from right) courtesy of the Museum of International Folk Art, a unit of the Museum of New Mexico, Santa Fe, NM. Pages 158-169: courtesy of El Rancho de las Golondrinas/Steven Mays.

Prop Credits

The Editors would like to thank the following for their courtesy in lending items for photography. Items not listed below are privately owned. Pages 38-39: antique furniture: Hepplewhite side chairs, Sheraton worktable, figural marble-top console table, Federal gilded wood and églomisé mirror—Bernard & S. Dean Levy, Inc., NYC; furniture motif watercolors and "The Five Senses" hand-colored engraving—Ursus Books and Prints, Ltd., NYC; antique silver creamer and waste bowl—S. J. Shrubsole, NYC; small gilded bronze bust on green marble base, deep yellow bowl and sugar bowl with brown appliqué, dinner plate with transfer figures and grape border, three-color marble plinth, blue French opalescent glass urn with gilded bronze mounts, cut crystal urn-shaped candlestick with swan motif bronze mounts, marble and slate plaque with allegorical scene, silk brocade table cover with knotted fringe, figural bronze candlestick on marble base—Vito Giallo Antiques, NYC; "Escorial" beige wool rug—ABC International Design Rugs, NYC; wallcoverings, "Tidewater Stripe" and "Stars" with coordinated "Stars Border," Williamsburg Small Prints Collection—Katzenbach & Warren, NYC. Page 67: all (except cabinet)—collection of the Hypertension Research Laboratory Foundation and Dr. M. Donald Blaufox.

Index

Acknowledgments

Our thanks to Dr. M. Donald Blaufox, Chris Clemens, Barbara Foss, Robert Frasch, Grace Friary of Historic Deerfield, Inc., Andrea Fritts of the Museum of Appalachia, Vito Giallo, Susan Hayden of the University Press of Kentucky, William H. Helfand, Rudy Herrera of El Rancho de las Golondrinas, Dorie Hoot of Genesee Country Museum, Alene Humphrey of the Museum of Appalachia, John Rice Irwin of the Museum of Appalachia, Loyal Jones, Bonnie and Chuck King, Bernard & S. Dean Levy, Inc., Paula Locklair of Historic Old Salem, Lannie Loeks, Jennifer Mange of Historic Deerfield, Inc., Bennie Moore, George Paloheimo of El Rancho de las Golondrinas, Delia Robinson of the Cobblestone Society of Albion, New York, Janine Skerry of Historic Deerfield, Inc., Beatrice M. Snyder of Hancock Shaker Village, Robert L. Stern of Historic Old Salem, Ed Weaver, Charles K. Wolfe, Philip Zea of Historic Deerfield, Inc., and Kenneth Zogry of Historic Old Salem for their help on this book.

First printing
Published simultaneously in Canada
School and library distribution by Silver Burdett Company,
Morristown, New Jersey

TIME-LIFE is a trademark of Time Incorporated U.S.A.

Production by Giga Communications, Inc.
Printed in U.S.A.

Library of Congress Cataloging-in-Publication Data

The Country Traveler
p.   cm. — (American country)
ISBN 0-8094-6795-X — ISBN 0-8094-6796-8 (lib. bdg.)
1. Villages—United States—Guide-books.
2. Historical museums—United States—Guide-books.
3. United States—Description and travel—1981- —Guide-books.
I. Time-Life Books. II. Series.
E161.C69   1990   917.304'928—dc20   90-31477
CIP

American Country was created by Rebus, Inc., and published by Time-Life Books.

REBUS, INC.

Publisher: RODNEY FRIEDMAN • Editor: MARYA DALRYMPLE
Executive Editor: RACHEL D. CARLEY • Managing Editor: BRENDA SAVARD • Consulting Editor: CHARLES L. MEE, JR.
Senior Editor: SUSAN B. GOODMAN • Copy Editor: ALEXA RIPLEY BARRE
Writers: JUDITH CRESSY, ROSEMARY G. RENNICKE • Freelance Writer: JOE L. ROSSON
Design Editors: NANCY MERNIT, CATHRYN SCHWING
Test Kitchen Director: GRACE YOUNG • Editor, The Country Letter: BONNIE J. SLOTNICK
Editorial Assistant: LEE CUTRONE • Contributing Editors: ANNE MOFFAT, DEE SHAPIRO,
KATE TOMKIEVICZ • Indexer: MARILYN FLAIG

Art Director: JUDITH HENRY • Associate Art Director: SARA REYNOLDS
Designers: AMY BERNIKER, TIMOTHY JEFFS
Photographer: STEVEN MAYS • Photo Editor: SUE ISRAEL
Photo Assistant: ROB WHITCOMB • Freelance Photographer: GEORGE ROSS
Freelance Photo Stylist: VALORIE FISHER

Series Consultants: BOB CAHN, HELAINE W. FENDELMAN, LINDA C. FRANKLIN, GLORIA GALE,
KATHLEEN EAGEN JOHNSON, JUNE SPRIGG, CLAIRE WHITCOMB

Time-Life Books Inc. is a wholly owned subsidiary of THE TIME INC. BOOK COMPANY.

President and Chief Executive Officer: KELSO F. SUTTON
President, Time Inc. Books Direct: CHRISTOPHER T. LINEN

TIME-LIFE BOOKS INC.

Editor: GEORGE CONSTABLE • Executive Editor: ELLEN PHILLIPS
Director of Design: LOUIS KLEIN • Director of Editorial Resources: PHYLLIS K. WISE
Director of Photography and Research: JOHN CONRAD WEISER

President: JOHN M. FAHEY JR.
Senior Vice Presidents: ROBERT M. DeSENA, PAUL R. STEWART, CURTIS G. VIEBRANZ, JOSEPH J. WARD
Vice Presidents: STEPHEN L. BAIR, BONITA L. BOEZEMAN, MARY P. DONOHOE, STEPHEN L. GOLDSTEIN,
JUANITA T. JAMES, ANDREW P. KAPLAN, TREVOR LUNN, SUSAN J. MARUYAMA, ROBERT H. SMITH
New Product Development: YURI OKUDA, DONIA ANN STEELE
Supervisor of Quality Control: JAMES KING
Publisher: JOSEPH J. WARD

For information about any Time-Life book please call 1-800-621-7026, or write:
Reader Information, Time-Life Customer Service
P.O. Box C-32068, Richmond, Virginia 23261-2068

Time-Life Books Inc. offers a wide range of fine recordings, including a Rock 'n' Roll Era series.
For subscription information, call 1-800-621-7026, or write TIME-LIFE MUSIC,
P.O. Box C-32068, Richmond, Virginia 23261-2068.